What people are saying about *The Journey* workbook:

The Journey *is a wonderful and worthwhile addition to the field of Violent Death Material. The current amount of material in this field is quite sparse and* The Journey *will prove to be valuable for professionals working with this population and for the co-victims as well.* The Journey *is unique in that the material can be used both in groups and individually and therefore will serve a multitude of purposes heretofore not available.*

Deborah Spungen, author of *And I Don't Want to Live This Life* and founder of Families of Murder Victims in Philadelphia

Connie Saindon has brought the theoretical into the practical with this user-friendly workbook for family and friends of those who have died traumatically. In addition, therapists and support group leaders will find many helpful tools here. Experiencing this workbook will help people move through their grieving journey with authenticity and eventually find themselves more resilient.

Janice Harris Lord, author of *No Time for Goodbyes: Coping with Sorrow, Anger, and Injustice After a Tragic Death* and former Director of Victim Services of Mothers Against Drunk Driving (MADD)

The Journey *workbook is a much needed and useful aid for adult survivors of violent death. Thoughtfully written, it respects the individual grieving process that each person goes through after having a loved one violently killed and offers specific tools to help calm the mind and body.*

Alison Salloum, PhD, LCSW, University of South Florida, College of Behavioral and Community Sciences

The Journey *is a wonderful tool not only for survivors of homicide, but survivors of suicide. I've not only had the privilege of taking* The Journey *training, but I have now facilitated two 10-week sessions. The change in participants from week 1 to week 10 is amazing; they become at peace after attending "The Journey." I have found that grief never ends, it changes;* The Journey *has taught me it's not a place to stay, but a place to remember who my loved one was. . . . I was so surprised how easy and simple this program is. I expected difficulty! I know I can do this and I'm ready! Thank you for the knowledge I have embraced from you! My calling is becoming a reality.*

Rose Madsen, Director of Families and Friends of Murder Victims, Inc.

I have found The Journey *to be very helpful in bringing healing and hope into the lives of those who have experienced a death of a family member to murder or suicide. Each time I have gathered together a group of people to support each other on The Journey, I have seen each person open themselves up to this very gentle and healing process.* The Journey *gives hope to broken hearts, and healing to hurting souls. It is so good to see smiles again! . . . Honestly, I dreaded this weekend. I knew I came without memory and felt that it would be a detriment. I dreaded the piece of the "work" that asked us to draw what we can't "let go." It intimidated me. Thank you for your genuineness, your gentleness, your understanding and acceptance. I look forward to growing our program here with your help and encouragement.*

Sr. Terry Maher, CPPS, BCC

Twenty-nine years ago my brother, Fred, was murdered. It forever changed my life. I had locked away the darkest memories because they were too painful. Every day as I awoke, the pain was right there. So I pushed them back further. I recently joined the 10-week support group called "The Journey" with the Diocese of San Bernardino. When this healing journey presented itself, I knew God was calling me. I opened my heart to the process and the Holy Spirit came in! I am so thankful to now have peace and to honor my brother by celebrating his life instead of only remembering his death.

JoAnn

This book is a wonderful learning tool. I plan to use this book often as I work with my group. This weekend has been such a good and healing experience. I could begin to feel my heart heal. Some darkness turned to light. The process we took has given me confidence. I feel more confidence to start my journey with a support group. Thank you.

Patricia Nelson

This experience is very powerful and empowering. It delves into the depths of the event, and into the core of my being. I believe that the exercises, even the difficult ones, are necessary steps in the healing process in an environment free of guilt and judgment. I enjoyed the laughter, and understand the tears—though painful memories came forth. I appreciate the grace, patience, sympathy and empathy in which the program is delivered. It has been insightful and helpful to me.

Anonymous

I was coming from a different perspective in my role of Diocese Director of Restorative Justice—because I wanted to see how the process works; to see if the volunteers present were really able to facilitate groups to see if the process would work for our Diocese both in English and Spanish. I took it as a wonderful process and it was a great weekend.

Sr. Sue Reif, OSF
Director of Restorative Justice
Diocese of San Bernardino

It was a very helpful experience. Before I came I was worried that this experience wouldn't translate well into Spanish, but it looks like it will translate well. Thank you so much. It was healing and affirming for me.

Anonymous

In the Thailand project with Hmong refugees, I could not have managed as well as I did without your training. Whenever I felt stuck by the moral and cultural obstacles we faced, I fell back on the techniques. . . . They were culturally resilient, relevant to the needs of the people, and dependable in bringing comforting care to the survivors of some of the most horrific (and ongoing) trauma I have encountered.

Jan Kujawa, in describing her work
with Doctors Without Borders

The Journey, a 10-week support group in the Diocese of San Bernardino, is a program I wish they had nine years ago when my daughter Melanie was killed. I did not know how to handle this tragedy so I held my feelings in and tried to keep life normal. By doing so I did a huge injustice to Melanie's sisters and myself. And now it is going on one year since my daughter Michelle was murdered. I knew I needed to deal with my grief and not make the same mistake twice. This program has brought joy and happiness back into my life. and I thank God for the precious time he allowed me to have with my daughters.

Linda

The Journey

Learning to Live with Violent Death

A Workbook
Based on *Restorative Retelling*

Connie Saindon, MA, MFT

Wigeon Publishing
San Diego

Wigeon Publishing
San Diego, California
www.WigeonPublishing.com

Second Edition: December 8, 2015

ISBN-10: 0989691381
ISBN-13: 978-0-9896913-8-3

Library of Congress Control Number: 2015919885

SEL010000: SELF-HELP / Death, Grief, Bereavement
FAM014000: FAMILY & RELATIONSHIPS / Death, Grief, Bereavement
PSY052000: PSYCHOLOGY / Grief & Loss

Edited by Larry M. Edwards

Cover design by Tim Brittain

Cover photo copyright © 2014 by Connie Saindon

Reflections About Time and Change by Dennis Klass
copyright 1983; used with permission

A Grief Like No Other by Kathleen O'Hara
copyright 2006; used with permission

Printed in the United States of America

The sale of this book supports programs for survivors of violent loss.
To obtain the book, go to:
http://svlp.org/resources/books.html

This book is dedicated to my sister Shirley Dianne "Tiny" Rollins, whose murder on December 8, 1961, led to this work. She lived her life giving to others, and it is my hope that this work will continue her life's intention.

Acknowledgements

My deepest appreciation for Marina, Austin, and Dee, and with this second addition, Myra, Louise, and Elena, who are the Survivor Voices answering the questions in this workbook. Their unselfish interest has been in helping others. It has been an honor to work with each of them.

Thanks also to Edward K. Rynearson for his review, support, and development of Restorative Retelling that provides the basis of this workbook.

The many families and survivors we have worked with have been both our clients and teachers. They ensure that a final book has not been written as there continues to be more to know. Without them we would not continue: I thank you for your continuing lessons and for keeping us on the path of helpfulness.

Editor Larry Edwards was exactly the right person for this project, and his insight, compassion, and expertise have been indispensible.

Funding for this project has been provided by Carmela Caldera, without whose generosity this work would not have been published.

Cover photo: This image was taken by the author at Mooselookmeguntik Lake, Rangely Lakes, Maine, in 2014.

Contents

Introduction

The Journey is a workbook for adults (and those who work with them) who have been impacted by violent death through homicide, suicide, terrorism, drunk driving, domestic violence, and war. Nationally, there are about 50,000 violent deaths annually. From that number, there are an additional ten to twelve people connected to the victim who are significantly impacted by this loss. These numbers do not take into account returning soldiers and their families who have been impacted by violent death as well.

This workbook not only provides important information about the complexities of violent death. Its main purpose is to offer a process to help shore up the resiliency of the readers as they live with a horrific loss. This self-help guide will be a resource for those who do not have access to specialists or those who may wish to strengthen their ability to live with what has happened more privately.

In the current literature, a workbook for professionals to use with clients or group participants who have been impacted by a violent death does not exist. This tool will be an aid to the clinician and client alike. The first edition was used as a facilitator's guide for ten-week support groups led by paraprofessionals or peers.

There are many circumstances whereby both the clinician and survivor may be overwhelmed with complex and often competing demands after a horrific loss. Previous training in trauma and grief is often inadequate for the many tasks that face them. There are a limited number of maps for professionals to use with their clients as they navigate the difficult journey ahead. Traditional ideas and methods may inadvertently increase distress with the kind of grief that does not go away with time. Clinicians may not specialize in violent loss and yet be asked for help sporadically in their practices or agencies. Requests for help may come years after the death of a loved one.

The Journey can aid professionals in offering services—services with which they are unfamiliar—in a more informed way. There are many locations that have adequate drop-in support groups for natural deaths, and there are national organizations that provide for monthly drop-in groups and advocacy surrounding criminal deaths. However, these groups do not specifically address a ten-week process to deal with unnatural deaths. This book is a useful adjunct to existing counseling, peer support, and advocacy.

Professionals will be guided through this process by using the Restorative Retelling Treatment Manual by Edward Rynearson, MD, which is available on the Violent Death Bereavement Society website. A three-year pilot study, in which this author was a contributor, showed a significant decrease comparing pre- and post-scores using this model. *The Journey* workbook will supplement the clinicians' manual for individual or group participants. There are now three more studies published in *Death Studies Journal, 2013-2014,* that continue to substantiate the work of the Restorative Retelling Model.

In *The Journey* workbook, readers are taken through a sequence of steps that build on one another. The process and accompanying documentation will be supported by the leading ideas in what helps in working with some of the aftermath of violent deaths. Quotations, research findings, and a bibliography of leaders in the field are included.

Throughout the workbook, questions will be asked to prompt the personal reporting of each reader as they are supported in knowing their reactions are normal for abnormal events. Images will help demonstrate the concepts, as it is well understood that losing someone in a violent way is often beyond words. The images will support and guide the reader in hearing the voices of other survivors who found value in the steps presented in the book.

Icons of Survivor Contributors who have found this process a vital path in their journey are also used. While the identity of the writers is protected by anonymity, the stories are their words and the icons are the actual symbols that each survivor has identified for remembering their loved ones.

Quotes and Facts are in sidebars and boxed text to highlight key concepts of leaders and researchers in this field.

Calming Strategies and poems close out each step. They will help connect the reader to the experiences of others and introduce calming strategies to manage intense emotions. The calming strategies and poems are written out at the end of each step as well as a companion audio format available as a download.

Resources are listed to guide the reader to books, websites, and organizations that can add to the information available to readers. This book recognizes fully that this publication is just one step in the reader's life-long journey.

Appendices contain supplemental information. There you will find support-group guide-lines, and more quotations, poems, and remembrance examples from Survivors.

Connie Saindon, MFT
Founder of Survivors of Violent Loss
San Diego, California

Alone No More

Alone no more.

Of all the goals of this workbook, the primary goal is to let you know that you are not alone. Whether you are a professional or a survivor, if this is all you discover in this workbook and nothing more, then we have succeeded in helping you in your Journey.

Alone no more is our hope this work will take you through steps that we have found help in this Journey that you have been delivered to. This is not travel that you and yours have selected, but one that has been, indeed, forced upon you.

> **The "We" that are included in this Journey with you are a collection of other survivors, both lay and professional, as well as victims whom you will find as contributors to your Journey. You will be introduced to survivors who will walk with you in this Journey in Step One.**
>
> **Read the section on contributors to see who else is there to be with you in your Journey. Many of them are survivors, too.**

You are invited to personalize and respond to this workbook with your experience. It can be a private account of your Journey or shared selectively or fully with others.

An audio component serves as a companion to this workbook. It has important calming exercises that guide you at the end of each step. Some of these exercises include a poem that may help you know your experience is shared by others as well. This material is available at the end of each step on your path. You may download an audio version at http://svlp.org/resources.html.

The Appendices include additional resources as well as a bibliography of publications, leaders in the field, online links, survivors' voices, heroes, and so forth.

There is no right or wrong answer—only a journey to reduce your isolation in this path to help you live better with what has happened to you.

How to Get the Most Out of This Workbook

WHAT YOU NEED TO GET STARTED Put your name in it and claim it as your book alone, and go back to it and add as more memories remind you of this process. Encourage others around you to get their own workbook and fill in their steps. Share it only with those who support you and you trust. You, unfortunately, are more the specialist in this process than most around you, no matter how professional or experienced they may be. You alone know your loved one and complexities that many can't come near knowing.

What you don't need is someone who will be critical of your process and remarks. If you can't find words in these steps, sketch or draw something that will show what you mean more accurately. This process so very often is beyond words, so have art (no, you don't have to be an artist to get the value out if this process) on hand to place in the book if you find it comforting and expressive for you. Find a quiet place where you won't be interrupted to be with us as we go on this Journey together.

WHAT THIS WORKBOOK IS NOT This workbook is not a substitute for professional services. It is quite likely that depression, post-traumatic stress and substance abuse are also a part of this Journey. Supplemental professional help is needed here and can be a great adjunct to your Journey. This workbook may be used in a support group as well. It is best used when the same group of people meet and go through the steps together. The steps will be most useful if completed in order. Each step builds on the preceding step.

These recommendations are only guidelines. What is more important is that you make the adjustments that fit you and your circumstances. There is no right way. You are in charge of your path. It is your Journey.

> *I have found that grief never ends, it changes. "The Journey" has taught me it's not a place to stay, but a place to remember who my loved one was.*
>
> Rose Madsen
> Director of
> Families & Friends
> of Murder Victims, Inc.

> *The first thing that comes to mind is that this has been a progressive experience for me. Having been involved with other ways of dealing with similar issues, they seemed to be focused on the tragedy and stayed stuck in that mode. In this process, each week I felt progress and positivism, and as a result felt lighter, freer, calmer and stronger.*
>
> Peggy, 8-26-99

Contributors

You are not alone!

You will be introduced to many survivors and professionals who will join you on this Journey. Contributors include the many victims that are represented by our Survivors and Professionals.

Violent loss impacts families and their worlds. Our contributors include members from many sectors of the community. Special acknowledgement goes to the many families we worked with directly at our Survivors of Violent Loss Program and Network. The Survivors of Violent Loss Program started in San Diego in 1998 with the effort of many.

Survivor Contributors include:

Marina, Dee, Chuck & Arlene, Cherry, Belisa, Ana, Kathy, Christie, Anna, Darlene, Nina, Kari, Anna, Michelle, Bonnie, Jackie, Larry, Kathy, Elena, Myra, Louise, and many more. Survivors will also be here in your Journey. Connecting with others is one of the major resources you will need to help you learn to live with what has happened to you. They represent losses of their parents, fathers, mothers, sisters, brothers, their children, nieces and nephews. They represent losses that are in all states.

Professional Contributors (many are survivors) include:

Ted Rynearson, MD; Stephen Shuchter, MD; Allison Salloum, PhD; Sid Zisook, MD; Deborah Spungen, MS; Janice Lord, MSW; Charles Moreau, MD; Meg Lawrence, MD; Jason Kornberg, MD; Robyn Aylor, PhD; Wendy Maurer, PhD, MFT; Yolanda Boyd; Coleen Dole, MSW; Coleen Marshall, MFT; Barbara Pimstein-Abala, MFT; Michelle Del Conte, PhD; Valerie Nash; Tom and Mary Ann Bennett; Cynthia Charlebois; Liz Munroe; Joyce Knott; Charlene Tate; Fred Will; Maggie Elvy; Charles Nelson, PhD; Maryanne Gallagher; Linda Pena; Paula Myers; Erik & Lisa Hoffacker; Chris Saindon, PhD; Joyce Knott and more.

They will be with you as you move along this path of ten steps.

Anonymous Survivor Writers:

The voices of other survivors will move along with you as you answer the questions. **You will find Survivors Writers included in each step answering the questions along with you.** They will be identified with icons that represent a memento that symbolizes a memory of their loved one.

We find remarkable resilience in everyone we work with. We continue to be amazed at what resources people have and can draw upon. Although wounded and changed forever by what has happened, they persevere and in time find ways to rebuild their lives. It is hoped that through their painful stories you will find inspiration for your own journey.

The Survivor Writers, like you are being asked to do, presented their true, spontaneous answers to the questions in this workbook. For obvious reasons, the survivor voices do not appear with their real names, and the details of their circumstances have been somewhat altered to protect their privacy. Nevertheless, each one's story is true in that behind each set of circumstances stands real persons with true events. They represent a small sampling of what happens and are not intended to represent the multitude of different situations.

Your answers to the questions will be your own. However, you may find that the Survivor Writers' answers resonate with you and your own story, and help you on your Journey.

Dee
Her niece was the first victim of a serial killer who killed five young women.

Elena
Her brother took his own life.

Marina
Her father's alleged killer was prosecuted, but the case ended in a mistrial and was never retried.

Myra
Her husband, a war veteran, took his own life.

Austin
His nephew, working as a photojournalist, was killed by police who retaliated against political protestors in Mexico.

Louise
Her husband was one of 53 killed in a missile-site disaster.

Connie
Lost her 17-year-old sister Tiny in 1961 in a small New England town.

The program is well thought out, the pace allows for introspection and reflection. My experience of it has come with great healing and I am most thankful. I am looking forward to working with the program and playing a part in helping to bring more healing to others.

Emma, 2015

About Pictures and Captions

BEYOND WORDS Losing someone in an unnatural way is beyond words. How does one speak of such a loss? We recognize that words often just don't do when it comes to speaking the *unspeakable*. Images can help say more clearly what has happened. (See the image in the sidebar.)

At the same time, an image can give us moments of focus on something that may be beautiful and perhaps calming. The image below has been donated by one of our survivors.

Cherry was robbed of her best friend and almost lost her life, but she did not lose Hawaii, where the crime occurred.

"Will I ever get over this?" is a question most survivors ask. We have found that folks don't "get over it," but they do learn to live with what has happened to them better. In time they find there is more space between the intense pain and some semblance of an everyday life.

Later on, you can read more on what other survivors said about their experiences. They can be your "virtual" group.

Some days you may want to protect yourself from reading more about other people's stories. You can choose when you want to read them.

Last September I learned that a close friend had lost her young son to a tragic accident thirty-five years ago. She couldn't figure out why she was still crying so many years later. I guess folks had uttered words about "moving on" and "finding closure" to her.

I made one of my inimitable, point-blank statements regarding the concept of closure. She liked it so much that she actually put it on a crock!

I thought it would look good on a T-shirt. She is a retired graphic artist and did me one better. Hope you like it—she sure did a beautiful job.

Marina

This workbook is just one place to help you manage the distress in your life. This is one way you can decide how much you want to take on.

Steps in this book will be most helpful if done sequentially. You may be back to visit and redo the steps periodically, but the first time around you may find it more helpful to do the steps in their order. Extra white space is provided intentionally for you to write or draw.

The Journey is moving you in a direction of increased management of what has happened to you. Our work with many family members tells us that this path has been successful for them and we hope it will be for you as well.

It is indeed quite normal to be overwhelmed with what has happened in a way that you may never have experienced before. You may indeed be consumed, feel possessed by what has happened.

If this isn't your experience you may be protecting yourself in order to provide support to other family members at this time.

In this new science of violent death bereavement, we know increasingly that the earlier you have support and a safe place to be with this loss, the greater opportunity there is in preventing a longer term health problems, including post-traumatic stress.

Research is new in its finding that violent loss bereavement can be even more painful and often involves symptoms of unremitting depression and PTSD.

Kaltman & Bonanno, 2003
Zisook, Chentsova-Dutton & Shuchter, 1998

Lack of predictability and controllability are central issues for the development and maintenance of PTSD.

Violent dying (from murder, suicide, or drunk driving) accounts for nearly 10% of annual deaths in the U.S., and may be associated with a prolonged bereavement in family members and friends.

The Story

Unfortunately, you have lost someone to a violent death and that is why you have this book. You may have become a member of a club that you never wanted to join. This is a very expensive club. You have paid the highest of dues, the ultimate price of the violent death of a loved one.

The loss of someone in an unnatural way is different than a natural death.

You are not alone. Violent death loss contributes to a large percentage of deaths worldwide. Although all deaths can be traumatic, the loss of someone from homicide, suicide, drunk-driving, or terrorist activities adds additional complexities that challenge family and community members.

This book exists to fill the gap with other resources that you may have. Each person should have their own book as the Journey is indeed quite personal, no matter how you are related to the person who died. Each of you has your own relationship and complexities to your loved one. This is the nature of human relationships. You may come together and use this book with supportive others. It may be a formal group or a group with family members, friends, or co-workers. It is important that all replies are accepted as true for the person sharing his or her experience. As you will notice, there are no right or wrong answers. A nonjudgmental approach will be an important guide in this process.

Each of you can share some or all of what you reveal in this workbook as your personal Journey. You may choose to work in this workbook alone as well. You decide what fits for you at this time. This

---

Unnatural Death

Ted Rynearson, MD, was the first and remains the leading theorist in violent death bereavement. He has helped us understand that when we lose some one in a violent way, it is different in these following ways:

Violent Death

1. It is Violent—a horrific death

2. It is a Violation—it is a wrongdoing

3. It is Volitional—it is an act done on purpose

4. And it is often Voyeuristic—public exposure by the news media

There really is a devil.

As told by the mother and sister of Becky, an honor-roll student killed by the wife of her first boyfriend, who she didn't know was married.

workbook is the first of its kind. You will hear from other survivors and specialists in the field; many are also survivors, like the author. What you reveal to others should be on your own timetable, when you wish to share. The violent loss of a loved one may leave you feeling overwhelmed and powerless. One way to have some power is to decide to whom and what you wish to say about your experience. In time, you may find out how others have done as well. We hear from so many that they felt so alone. Hearing from others reduces that sense of "I am the only one this happened to."

Most of what you experience you will find is quite normal, that it is a normal reaction to an abnormal event. Many of us have had other losses from natural ways. Deaths from illness and disease, some accidents, and, of course, the natural deaths due to aging that we will all face ourselves.

Violent loss is different and the traditional way of thinking and coping with loss may not help.

In an unnatural death, there is:
— No time for good-byes
— No time to prepare
— A problem understanding the way they died
— A violation of you and your loved one
— No choice

> *There is no way that the violent dying of a loved one can end with meaning, only an empty absurdity. This never should have happened.*
>
> **Edward K. Rynearson, MD**

Review the sidebar on the previous page, which points out some of those ways that violent loss is different from losing a loved one in a natural way.

Next, read the calming exercise for Step One at the end of this section, or listen to the downloadable audio recording. Remember, the calming exercise is there for you to listen to at anytime as you travel on this Journey. You will be directed to read or listen to it at the end of each step, but begin with it now. After you're done, begin answering the questions for Step One.

Many who have had a criminal death also report the occurrence of "second injuries."

Examples include:

- When co-victims are blamed for not preventing what happened.

- When the legal system does not give them a role.

- Courts seem to treat criminals better than victims.

- Family members are treated and considered suspects.

Symonds, 1982

Unplugged from LIFE
By Kathy, whose sister was murdered

STEP ONE, QUESTION ONE

Have you lost someone in a natural death?

Yes_____? No_____?

If you answered yes, your next question is:

Does the loss that is the focus of your Journey in this workbook differ? If so, what words or images relay that difference for you? Write your answer here or in a separate notebook.

The Suicide Crisis

1. There's a suicide in the U.S. every 13 minutes.

2. Americans are more likely to kill themselves than each other.

3. Each suicide costs society $1 million in medical and loss-of-work expenses.

4. 40,000 suicides annually.

Gregg Zoroya
USA Today
10-11-14

Murder Rate

The FBI reports (2010) that . . . a person is murdered every 35.6 minutes in the United States of America.

Restorative Retelling

Restorative Retelling intervention is designed to moderate internalized trauma and separation distress.

Phyllis Rogers, MA, LMHC
Director, inLife Clinic
Chaplain, Redmond Police
and Fire Departments

If you found that yes, there are significant differences in your experience, you are certainly not alone. Survivors like yourself, as well as researchers who have studied this area, have found that coming to terms with losing someone to violent death requires specialized approaches.

Some of the contributing leaders introducing new ideas regarding violent loss are professionals who also have had violent losses in their families. They are members of your club, too.

Ted Rynearson, MD, the leader in homicidal bereavement, tells of the violent loss of his wife in his book, *Retelling Violent Death*. Deborah Spungen writes about the loss of her daughter in *And I Don't Want to Live This Life*. Connie Saindon, the author of this workbook and founder of the Survivors of Violent Loss Program and website, describes the loss of her sister. All of them will be part of your team on this Journey you will take, with this workbook as your guide.

The voices of other survivors will move along with you as you answer the questions. **Each one is anonymous and identified with an icon that represents a memento that symbolizes a memory of their loved one. See Step Ten for the meaning for each icon.**

Survivor Voices

STEP ONE, QUESTION ONE

Dee
My experience of losing a loved one to a more natural death is that it was expected; i.e., old age, illness. There was Time to process the coming event, Time to say good-bye, Time to let go, Time to say many things, time to spend extra time being with that person, Time to be a part of your loved ones ultimate transition, Time to comfort. Time, Time, Time.

My experience of losing my loved one to her violent death was that I had an inability to comprehend the information being given to me, disbelief, and non-acceptance. Then . . . horrific images of loss, sudden total physical & mental sadness to the depth of my being; my need for information—all information and there was none; having to have reaffirmation that this has really happened—really, Guilt, no Time to process, no Time to say good-bye, no Time to prevent, no Time to comfort, no Time to protect. All Time is gone forever—No Time, No Time, No Time. All is Empty. My Soul is Empty. Cannot function on the simplest level. Cannot stop crying for what seems like forever. My Soul is Empty.

Elena
Yes, I have lost 3 people very close to me to "natural" death (two to cancer and one to congestive heart failure).

Yes, death by suicide is totally different. It is the difference between sorrow and terror, letting go and being ripped apart. It is the difference between a heavy heart and a shattered one. In losing my brother to suicide, everything I thought I knew about life was turned upside down. I questioned everything I once held dear and I embraced the people and beliefs I once took for granted.

My physical responses in natural death were tears and a need to be held by those around me that I loved. My response to my brother's death by suicide was intensely visceral. Every bit of my body was suddenly filled with pain, especially my arms, which ached terribly and my chest, which felt as if my heart had been ripped out and all that remained was a huge hole that could hold the Grand Canyon itself. And my chest felt so cold, I couldn't get warm and stop shivering. There were no arms in this world large enough to hold that pain, and I felt so very alone in it.

 **Marina**
I had experienced natural death prior to my father's murder. Natural death is sad. Painful. If the death is a result of a chronic disease, it can be exhausting and seemingly open-ended, up until the end. Violent death, on the other hand, comes with a raft of unwelcome and life-threatening side-effects. Where do I start? I was blind-sided. The fact of murder just didn't fit into my previous experience in any way.

 **Myra**
My father died four years after my husband. I could not believe the difference between the two deaths. When my father died, I expected it to be the rollercoaster of my husband's death. There was sadness and stress at dealing with writing an obituary that would have made him proud, but there were no panic attacks, no questions, no guilt, no feeling out of control. I went through the funeral with sadness at his passing, knowing I would forever be without my father, but he was 87 and went quickly. When people asked about my father, it was easy to tell them he passed from natural causes (pneumonia).

My experience of losing my loved one to her violent death was that I . . . cannot function on the simplest level. Cannot stop crying for what seems like forever. My Soul is Empty.

Dee

In losing my brother to suicide, everything I thought I knew about life was turned upside down.

My physical responses in natural death were tears and a need to be held by those around me that I loved.

Elena

Where do I start? I was blind-sided. The fact of murder just didn't fit into my previous experience in any way.

Marina

My husband's death was a suicide, the reaction when people find that out is always stressful and is still stressful. I had been married for thirty years and did not know how to do many things.

Myra

My husband's death was a suicide; the reaction when people find that out is always stressful and is still stressful. I had been married for thirty years and did not know how to do many things. I had the pressure of a job, the house that was left unfinished (it was under remodeling), and grieving. With my dad's passing, I had my life together and all I dealt with was his passing.

Austin
This loss is quite different. In the natural deaths in my family and for close friends, there was a "warning" that those individuals might or were going to die. Even with my father, who committed suicide, there was a warning. My mother had told us that Father had a heart condition and that he may not be around long. Though the suicide was not foretold. Word images would include: shock, tragedy, disbelief, sorrow, hurt, anger and sympathy.

Louise
At the time, no person in my family that I was close to had died. My 28-year-old husband was the first. Even today, 50 years later, death seems so sudden and final, even if it is expected. Every individual person who dies leaves a gap in my life. Everyone makes a difference.

Connie
I don't think I thought about it much until the time in my life that I wanted to work with those who had lost someone the way I had lost my sister. As I reviewed the literature regarding homicide bereavement, I found so little. What I did find didn't fit what I understood personally nor professionally. At that time, 1997, what I understood was that in grief you went through stages, then you got "got over it" and went on with your life. I knew the experience of the loss of my sister was different and the people I worked with taught me that as well. I realized that if I didn't think that, then there was certainly something wrong with me and everyone I knew who had lost someone in a violent way. In my search for someone who seemed to describe what I intuitively knew, I found, with my son's help, the work of Ted Rynearson, MD. His articles on homicidal bereavement were indeed refreshing and gave me hope for the first time that I may be able to understand this kind of loss to not only help me but to be of aid to others with a similar loss.

STEP ONE, QUESTION TWO

What happened in your life that has you a member of this club you never wanted to join? What happened? How were you notified?

Please describe as much or as little as you can, or bring forth news items that can say what has happened.

You may wish to visit this question again when you are able to describe more of what happened. There is value in using your own words or images that describe your experience; however, we fully acknowledge the difficulty in doing so. So, to begin, just tell what happened to your world that you are now a member of the Survivors Club.

As I mentioned, you are not alone. Together with you in this question are the responses of your workbook team. When you are ready, perhaps after you have answered each question, read the voices of other survivors and their stories in each section.

You are encouraged to use this page for writing your story or keeping notes. Or place news articles here, or draw images that speak about what has happened. Make this as long or short as you wish. More space is available on the following page, or use a notebook or extra paper, if you need to.

Survivor Voices

STEP ONE, QUESTION TWO

 **Dee**
What happened to have me become a member of a club that I never wanted to be a member of? On December 21st of 1984, my 20-year-old niece (who came into my life when I was 12 years old) was viciously murdered. We were very close. She was alone at a friend's house late at night studying for her college finals after meeting with friends to celebrate Christmas, exchange gifts and sing carols. We now know that she heard a disturbance outside and opened the door to look out. A man who was high on drugs and alcohol was screaming at the sky as he made his way down the street and when he saw my niece, he rushed to force his way into the small house. He violently stripped her, beat her until she was unrecognizable, bound her with electrical cord, raped her and repeatedly stabbed her to death.

Her death went unsolved for 14 years until 1999 when her case and 2 other unsolved cases in the area were re-opened. With new forensic technology, one man was linked to all three cases and he was arrested just prior to his being released from parole for the murder of another young woman whom he had known. He had been sentenced to 35 years for her murder, but had served just 12. When arrested, he confessed to a 5th victim in a nearby area. All five murders occurred within an 18-month period. My niece was his first known victim.

In 1984, this event forever changed the pattern of my family's lives. My family fragmented. Over a short period of time, a family business was lost partly because of the mental effect the murder had on my father; my parents divorced. My grandmother, with whom my niece had lived at the time of the murder, passed away 3 years later, never really having recovered from losing her first great-grandchild with whom she was so close. You are not supposed to outlive your great-grandchildren, she had said. The effects of this event on me, I believe, contributed to my marriage ending in 1989.

My work with restorative retelling has helped me understand that after a violent loss, one has not only the familiar separation distress that occurs in natural dying, but also trauma distress, which has more to do with how a loved one dies.

Connie Saindon

This loss is quite different. In the natural deaths in my family and for close friends, there was a "warning" that those individuals might or were going to die.

Austin

PTSD is more severe and longer lasting when the trauma is of human design.

BUET & SMUCKER, 2006

Fortunately, when the case was solved in 1999, I found the Survivors of Violent Loss Program—having been formed one short year earlier. The group helped me in coming to terms with these effects and also in preparing for trial later that year. How different things would have been had I not been in those groups. The murderer was sentenced to death for my niece's death and sits on death row. He awaits word on his last appeal to overturn the death penalty and commute it to life. The judge had 2 years to rule on his statement. We waited.

After 8 more years of appeals, totaling 16 years since the defendant's sentencing, we have suffered through new court rulings, a court order stating that a new Sentencing Trial be given to the defendant or else commute his death sentence to Life. This may lead to more appeals, then reversal of the prior ruling, more appeals, back and forth from Federal to State Courts on different levels, and the process just goes on and on. It is a weary process.

This process gives his life purpose. I want his life to have no purpose. He took that away from my niece who hoped to become a doctor, and also from the subsequent four women who fell victim to him.

I have the support and understanding of the Survivors of Violent Loss Group. I will never be without it. It is within me.

Elena
My brother had been away in Europe on a business trip for 2 weeks. He had been very angry and argumentative for a few months before he left, but he had called me just before his trip and had sounded excited about life again and hopeful. He was due home that weekend, and I was looking forward to speaking with him.

I received a phone call from my mother asking me to come home right away. She sounded terribly upset and wasn't making any sense. Then Dad came on the line and finally told me my brother had shot himself the same night he was back

Survivor Kathy shows her burden this way . . .

home, which was Seattle, Washington. We lived in Southern California and had only received a police notification so there were many questions.

Later we learned that he had not let a woman he was serious about know he was coming home in order to surprise her, but instead he found her with someone else.

He went home and began drinking heavily. It was raining, and I know that my brother hated that aspect of Seattle, that it rained so much. He shot himself in his house, at his office desk, in the night.

Marina

My dad was bludgeoned and strangled by his girlfriend. She was and still is a grifter and predator who had a pattern of finding wealthy older men, locking them into sexual relationships, and then demanding money or material goods. Unbeknownst to me, she physically abused my father for five years. She murdered him because he was ending the relationship. I cannot adequately describe the intense physical and mental anguish I experienced when I learned of the murder. I felt tremendous rage, guilt, and despair. I was no longer part of the world. Instead, I was a pariah. Shortly after the coroner's deputy informed me that my father had been murdered, I realized that there would be a trial, and that I would have to see the individual who had selfishly taken Dad's life. The time of waking and sleeping nightmares began. I was helpless to stop it.

Myra

My husband was a Vietnam War vet. He did two tours in the army in Vietnam and this part of his life continually impacted him. The V.A. diagnosed him with PTSD. He never went for help and said that PTSD was for weak people.

He was estranged from his family and had issues with employment. He was self-employed as a mason. He was very artistic and loved working for people who wanted the artistic flair that he embraced.

Though suffering itself is universal, each experience of suffering is unique because each person who goes through it is unique. Who the self was before the loss makes each person's experience different from all others.

That is why suffering loss is a solitary experience. That is also why each of us must ultimately face it alone. No one can deliver us, substitute for us, or mitigate the pain in us.

But loss does not have to isolate us or make us feel lonely. Though it is a solitary experience we must face alone, loss is also a common experience that can lead us to community. It can create a community of brokenness. We must enter the darkness of loss alone, but once there we will find others with whom we can share life together.

Sittser, 1996

My husband had been drinking more and more over the years. He was a beer drinker who eventually went to vodka. He was able to handle a lot of liquor and still seem fine. He sometimes seemed depressed, but would always pull out of it. He loved his dog, and he loved his house and the projects around the house. He loved camping, boating, fishing, and loved our long vacations.

We were scheduled to leave for our camping vacation in September, for three weeks. He always had our supplies organized, the van packed, the boat ready. The day before he took his life was his birthday. He had just turned 59. Two days before he said, "I am going to play through." I didn't get what that meant at the time. He was more and more agitated about the political situation in our country, upset with the cable company, and everything irritated him, yet he was talking a lot about our trip.

I returned from getting materials for our trip. In the next thirty minutes he went from being alive to shooting himself in the head. It was completely unexpected and the experience left me with all of the guilt, questions, and sadness that a suicide brings.

Austin
My nephew was murdered in Mexico.

Louise
My husband was killed along with many others when there was a huge explosion in a missile silo. My husband was on a team making a circuit to test and update missile site equipment around the United States. This was the second missile site on the tour. One afternoon everyone had gone out of the site for lunch and someone inadvertently did not completely close an oxygen tank valve when he left. After lunch, when everyone was back to work, someone turned on a piece of equipment that sparked and the oxygen that had leaked out instantly exploded. Everyone, or nearly everyone, in the silo was killed. Th cause of death was said to be a concussion from the force of the explosion. When I viewed my husband's body it was not burned, so I assume any fire was quickly put out.

At the time, I was at home with my two children and didn't have the TV on until the wife of another member of the team came over to my house. I didn't know her. Soon another wife appeared, then another. By that time the TV was on and reports of the accident were being covered. Other women came over, some of them bringing food. It did not even occur to me that this might mean they knew something I didn't know about what had happened, but I remember wondering why they were all coming to my house, since I didn't know them. In a few hours, my husband's supervisor on the job came and took me in the kitchen and told me the news. I can't remember his name, what he said, or what I said, just that he put his arms around me in a comforting gesture. I didn't question if it was true, or any details; I just was in shock mostly. The telephone rang and it was my husband's parents calling long distance. They had seen the news and wanted to know if he was involved. When I said, "Yes," that he had been killed, I think his mother fainted and his dad came on the phone. I don't remember the rest of the conversation.

Later, I got a call from the mortuary saying I could come view his body. I had never seen a dead body, had never been to a funeral, did not really know what I was supposed to do. I went down and saw my husband, embalmed. I just didn't have any feelings, I was in a daze.

Connie

I became a member of this club in 1961. My sister lost her identity and became: DEAD BLONDE IN GRAVEL PIT, as the detective magazine labeled her.

It was a cool December morning, December 8 in fact, just after I had married. My sister was walking to catch a ride to her last day of classes to complete her beauty school training. Coats were a must for this time of the year. My brother Bill remembers seeing her walking her usual route to catch her ride to a city 40 miles away. She'd told him earlier that she had a toothache, but was not staying home as she was graduating from Beauty College that day. Dad passed her on the road that morning. He can still see her smiling and waving at him. He knows she'd still be alive, if he had only stopped and given her a ride. Overwhelming guilt continued to plague him all his life.

Instead of him giving her a ride, an acquaintance, someone she'd met just a couple of times, offered her a ride that chilly morning in Maine. She was so happy, as was her nature, but that day was more special because of the graduation. He needed to find a part for his boat and there was time to look for it at the local dump. Some say she laughed at him because his car wouldn't start. He stabbed her and when she tried to get out of his car he hit her head with a brick. She died 10 minutes away from the hospital after being found by a couple of workmen, who drove her to the hospital.

Now it is time to listen to Step One of the audio component that accompanies this workbook, or you may read a copy of the text. There are ten exercises recorded, one for each step. The corresponding exercise is found at the end of each of the ten steps.

You may download an audio version at http://svlp.org/resources.html.

Step One Closing Exercise

Comforting Heart Breathing Exercise

To get ready for this experience, sit in a comfortable chair in a quiet place where you will not be interrupted . . . then place your feet flat on the floor. . . . Sit forward and lean back with your shoulders resting on the back of your chair. You may discover that you are sitting in a slant with your buttocks closer to the edge of your chair leaning back. (You may also lie down to do this.)

Place your hands on the upper part of your chest . . . gently, one on top of the other . . . and begin first by just noticing . . . the weight of your hands resting on your chest. . . . Make sure that your arms are not resting on the arms of the chair to get the full feel of the weight of your hands on your chest. . . . Now . . . notice the slight movement of your hands from your own breathing. . . .

You may find that closing your eyes helps you to focus more on these slight sensations. Again . . . notice the slight movement of your hands from your own breathing. . . . You may also notice your heartbeat. . . . Just notice this for a few moments. . . . Make sure that your elbows are not resting on the chair, that they are free. . . . Notice, again, the weight of your hands on your chest . . . resting gently. Notice the rise and fall of your chest from your own breathing.

*Now . . . take a deep breath in through your nose and **hold it** . . . . for as long as you can . . . and when you are ready . . . form your mouth into an O . . . and slowly breath out . . . let that air go . . . all the way out. . . . Then relax . . . and . . . slump . . . keeping your hands in place . . . just slump . . . like a rag doll . . . letting those muscles go . . . and relax . . . notice how well that chair is supporting you . . . with nothing you need to do . . . no place to go . . . you can just to let go . . . and relax.*

It is important NOT to do these deep breaths one right after the other. You may experience dizziness if you do. Do normal breathing in between the deep breaths.

You may discover that your breathing is very short; breathing with this practice activity will be an asset to your overall health and increase deeper breaths. It is a self-soothing, calming technique.

Take another deep breath and hold it for as long as you can, and then . . . form your mouth into an O . . . and slowly breath out . . . let that air go . . . all the way out. . . . Then relax . . . and . . . slump . . . keeping your hands in place . . . just slump . . . like a rag doll . . . letting those muscles go . . . and relax. . . .

We are all born with the ability to calm and soothe ourselves, and this exercise calls upon this ability to help counterbalance and manage what has happened to you. Scientific research on self-soothing strategies, such as meditation and this kind of focused deep breathing, found that these strategies work by fooling the brain into perceiving the world as not so threatening, so the brain sends out hormones and electrical signals telling the body to relax.

These changes counterbalance the fight/flight response when we are alarmed and under stress.

Take another deep breath and hold it for as long as you can, and then . . . form your mouth into an O . . . and slowly breath out . . . let that air go . . . all the way out. . . . Then relax . . . and . . . slump . . . keeping your hands in place . . . just slump . . . like a rag doll . . . letting those muscles go . . . and relax. . . .

When our heart rate and breathing slow down . . . it neutralizes the harmful effects of stress on our system. And . . .

The following benefits may occur:

— Stronger immune system
— Improved memory and attention
— Decreased blood pressure
— Decreased symptoms of depression and anxiety
— Increased alertness
— Controls binge eating
— Lowers blood sugar

To improve and practice the power of breathing . . . practice by taking deep breaths in and holding them for as long as you can, in and out of your day . . . one at a time, with normal breaths in between deep breaths.

Take your time to come back to the experience of being in the room you are in . . . notice where you are . . . knowing you have strengthened your ability to feel lighter for a few moments of your day. . . .

STEP TWO

Sources of Support

How are you doing so far with the Journey you are taking in this workbook? We have asked you to tell what happened to you that resulted in you being a member of the Survivors Club. You may wish to read the stories of others who have a story that resulted in their membership as well. Read the stories that follow in Survivor Voices. Is it difficult to hear other stories?

Sources of Support

An important question at this juncture is to identify and refer back to who is available to you for support. Your Journey includes meeting new folks who have an interest in what has happened for various reasons. The complexity of your story

will call upon a variety of folks in your community; such as, medical, legal, media, mental health and so on. Our interest in this section is for you to first identify who is there when you need to cry, be quiet, ask questions, vent, remind yourself to do everyday tasks, and so on. Recognize that sources of support may change as well. People who may have had great advice before seem to miss the mark. People who blame you or seem to know what you should do may be less helpful now and stand out. This is your time to move toward those who are truly a resource and away from those who add to your distress.

Confusion permeates— friends and family do not know what to do or say.

There is no such thing as normal; normal is a setting on a washing machine.

Co-victim

The Journey involves re-building, finding a new normal; that is re-setting your life. The path is often from being a victim to becoming a survivor and then a thriver.

Deborah Spungen

Although you may not want to be a member of any club that identifies you with what has happened, you may relate to the term.

Co-victim

Just come sit with me on my Mourning Bench.

"Lament for a Son" by Nicholas Wolterstorff

This page intentionally left blank. You are encouraged to use it for writing your story or keeping notes.

STEP TWO, QUESTION ONE

Who is there for you? Please list their names, and how they have been supportive to you. There are usually surprises. Have there been some people you didn't think would be there for you and some that have not?

Survivor Voices

STEP TWO, QUESTION ONE

Dee

In 1984, when Tara was murdered in Texas, I lived in Colorado with my husband, Bob, and my young children Scott, Jessica, and Dale, ages 11, 6, and 2. I was working and my co-workers were sympathetic and concerned. My family of origin was in Texas. I believe I was in shock, but sought no medical help or therapy and no one suggested it to me. I like to think that my husband and I supported each other the best we could. Honestly, there is much I cannot recall.

In 1999, when the case was solved, I was divorced and living in San Diego. It felt like the scab was torn off, painful as ever. My two oldest were pretty much starting out on their own, my youngest living with his dad. Bob was remarried and living in San Diego also with his wife, Jo Jo. I remember telling him the news and it seemed painful for him in more ways than one, and he simply could not be of support to me under the existing circumstances. The wounds were re-opened for my children as well. My biggest support comes from my close group of friends I have found here. They surround me. Through them I was led to find SVLP. Individual counseling with Connie helped immeasurably. Working through the SVLP groups helped me the most. My co-workers are very supportive and my employers allowed me time off to attend the trial in November 2000. I was attending the SVLP group for Preparing for Trial that November and, to my surprise and appreciation, each participant wrote a few words of encouragement on paper hearts and strung them on a necklace for me to wear at the trial to show their support for me, to hold them close. What a difference.

Elena

My husband was very supportive in that he took charge of the children and many of the errands/responsibilities I was too overwhelmed to deal with at the time. I don't know how I would of gone through that time without his quiet strength.

I also developed an unexpected relationship with a few people from my church community with whom I could share my story and be heard without judgment. They also had a gift for calling and checking up on me periodically, not saying much but being present. But I did not feel comfortable burdening them with my thoughts.

An especially important support for me was that I began to meet with a spiritual director regularly. This was about six years after my brother's death. It is with her that I was really able to share a great deal of a story that seemed too heavy or too old for others to have to hear about.

Marina

Four people were there for me. They were: John, who was my significant other at the time of the murder. He came from a religious tradition that emphasizes unwavering support in the face of hardship. He really lived it after Dad's murder. He was a quiet presence by my side from Day One. He was as shocked and stymied as I was by the initial fact of the murder itself. As time went on, he was simply there. He asked how I was doing several times every day, or whenever I seemed to need it. He changed the locks on Dad's house after the police advised us to do so. He shepherded me to the rosary service, and made sure I somehow got through the funeral, and subsequent memorial. During the first year or two, he called from work several times a day to confirm that I had not fallen off the edge of the Earth. He knew I like to be alone a lot, and gave me plenty of space to grieve and process things in my own way. He was a fairly taciturn sort, but at the worst moments he found the words that somehow cut through the agony, the bewilderment, and the numbness . . . words that led me unfailingly to the next step in my journey as a survivor. I never, ever had the sense that he would walk away. His utter constancy was his greatest gift to me.

My best friend, Laura, was a life saver. Her sister Chris pitched in more than once. They helped me get through those twilight days in the simplest of ways. Soon after the murder, they came to my house for a swim and a barbecue. We ate steak and shrimp. We gobbled See's Candies. They filled entire boxes with my favorite milk-chocolate butter creams and Kona Mochas. We swam and talked. They gave me plenty of space when I needed to be quiet. During the visit, I received the call from the coroner's deputy on the cause of death. I sigh deeply when I remember the unthinkable words, "Manual strangulation with attendant blunt-force trauma to the head, face, and back of the neck." I congratulated myself from some far-away corner of my mind for my ability to remain standing in the face of such information. Laura and Chris praised me as well. Later, they sat on either side of me as I cried piteously. They held my hands, stroked my back, and murmured soothing words. They never wavered. Not once.

Another friend, Peggy, is a Himalayan guide. She insisted that I come to visit her in San Francisco three weeks after the murder. I was ravenous, as I exercised strenuously in order to calm myself. She fed me good food, and took me to beautiful, timeless places in Big Sur and Carmel. We hiked, and went to a barn dance with rough-hewn cowboys. Everyone at the dance had been told about the murder in advance. With only one exception, everyone seemed to understand that it was important to make sure that I was fed, warm, and not forgotten. A cowboy coaxed me out onto the dance floor. I was pretty messed up inside, but the music suffused me with joy and energy. I danced and danced. I'll never forget how that old cowboy's lined, rugged face lit up with pleasure at the sight of my ear-to-ear grin. I felt so fortunate and grateful to be alive and breathing.

Finally, my Amazon parrots Gideon, Philo, and Paquita were incredible. They were a great comfort to me. Their intelligence, sensitivity and playfulness helped to remind me of the good things in life. Taking care of them helped me to live in the moment, and prevented me from drifting off into the abyss. Stroking their soft feathers and scratching their heads gave me profound pleasure, even as I experienced the worst pain of my life.

Myra
1. The team at hospice was my saving grace. The medical examiner made that connection for me and kept calling to make sure I found help. My therapist was my lifeline, and without her I would probably not be here today.

39

2. *My husband's best friend was my other lifeline. He took me to dinner, called me daily and took me to events. He got me involved in music and got my violin out of storage and signed me up for lessons. This became my other lifeline.*

3. *My school friends invited me for dinner every Tuesday, since that was the night he died.*

4. *My mom was a great support and made sure I went away every break for a vacation, just as my husband and I had done.*

5. *My college roommates knew how little I knew about cooking and shopping. They taught me to cook and grocery shop.*

Austin
When my nephew was murdered I was already involved in SVLP and had been reading Dr. Rynearson's book. I also had a support system from the SVLP Board and members. Connie Saindon has been the greatest support.

Louise
I called my own parents, in California, getting them out of bed. Dad answered and relayed the news to my mother. He said he would come. My sister also came from California. They must have flown and arrived the next day. There were still wives and company people at my house. Someone called a doctor and he came and gave me some kind of shot that made me sleep. It was all kind of a blur. I don't remember taking care of my 3-½-year-old daughter or 9-month-old-son. I guess my sister filled in for me for what I didn't/couldn't do.

The wives came over and packed up all the furniture and belongings; the company arranged for them to be put in storage in Escondido, where my parents lived.

All of my husband's relatives came to the funeral. I didn't take my children—I didn't think I could take care of them at the funeral, and they were awfully little for such a thing.

My dad and I and the two kids set out driving to California.

My sister will listen as often and as long as I need to talk. Her philosophy is do what you need to do, whenever you need to do it. Stop when you need to.

My brother will call, ask how I am, listen, put in his ideas as the conversation flows. He is a minister of like mind to me.

My daughter will express empathy if I am feeling down and tell her so. She is very kind-hearted.

My sons will call to check on how I am, listen, empathize if things aren't going well, offer assistance and presence, and assure me that it is natural to feel what I feel.

A male friend who has survived a violent loss will listen, share experiences, be honest and open.

I don't tell many people about this part of my past. There are other people who would listen and let me talk and be understanding if I told them what happened.

Connie

No one knew how to deal with this. My parents' marriage, already weakened from years of disagreements, fell apart. This new crisis took the focus off the death of my sister, which no one knew how to deal with anyway. The best we all could do was deal with it like any other death. I quickly began to organize and take care of things (a trait I have today). I remember picking out my sister's dress that she would be buried in. It was the dress she wore at my wedding just a few days before.

There were no victim assistance programs in place. No crisis teams. The thing to do then was not to talk about it. So my joining my new husband in Puerto Rico helped me do that. I put "it" in a box that I didn't open again until over thirty years later. In visits home, I was criticized for bringing "it" up again. "It" only upsets people.

This page intentionally left blank. You are encouraged to use it for writing your story or keeping notes.

STEP TWO, QUESTION TWO

What do you believe happens after someone dies? Is your belief a source of comfort? What you believe may add to your distress or be called upon to comfort you.

Survivor Voices

STEP TWO, QUESTION TWO

Dee

I believe in an afterlife. I believe I am a spiritual being having an earthly experience. I believe there is a place—heaven, the "other side"—that is not so far away. I believe we go there when we depart this life and that we are reunited with friends and loved ones. These thoughts comfort me greatly. Separation is never easy in this life. Losing someone in death has long-lasting effects. Everything is changed. My faith in a God Source and my belief that we are all forever connected gives me a sense of peace and comfort.

Elena

I believe that when we die our being encounters the one who created us as body and being. I believe that at the moment our being begins to grasp all that we could not understand when we physically lived in this world. I believe our creator holds us lovingly and listens to us as a gentle father does with a child, and just loves us. I believe there will come a time when our being and body will reunite and be able to live out the full realization of being loved without confusion or suffering. This is a source of great comfort and hope for me.

Marina

I am an atheist. I do not believe in an afterlife, nor do I believe in Heaven or Hell. Plenty of both right here on Earth. No need to look elsewhere for them. I believe that when I die, that's it. End of story.

Arriving at my belief system involved a long, arduous process that began when I was still a very young child. It involved a lot of thought and work. Plenty of pain, too, as I was frequently subjected to the abusive disapproval of those close to me. Still I persisted. I even took elective courses in Christian archaeology, philosophy, and biblical

I believe that as a biological organism, I have only one life to live. Therefore, I must endeavor to live in the present.

Marina

I believe that we will see each other again and that he is at peace in his new world.

Myra

I am an atheist. I do not believe in an afterlife, nor do I believe in Heaven or Hell. Plenty of both right here on Earth. No need to look elsewhere for them. I believe that when I die, that's it. End of story.

Marina

literature at the rigorous Jesuit university I attended. My atheism was not arrived at casually or easily. I do not take it lightly, and I guard it with all of the quiet integrity I can muster.

That said, I do admire Buddhism and Daoism. Buddhism in particular is not a god-centered religion. Its tenets suit me well. Its emphasis on wisdom and compassion, emotional detachment, and lack of attachment to desire or outcome are vital in helping me to cope.

Between my atheism, and the aforementioned Eastern traditions, I was able to accommodate the finality of my father's death. I continually reminded myself to be grateful that I was alive and healthy, even as I muddled painfully through the days. Of course, atheism was of no comfort when my thoughts turned to the fate of the woman who murdered my father. Nor did it help when she got off after a mistrial. I'll never forget her smug triumph as she faced me outside the courtroom.

I wanted to die. This creature was surrounded by women from her church. They didn't even know her before the murder. She was not a friend to women, as she tended to go after their men. I will never forget how her counterfeit companions leaned forward avidly as I stared at my father's killer. They resembled hyenas, thirsting for my blood, tissue, and bone. Their hunger for my helpless anguish shocked me to the core.

I do not believe that my father's murderer will be judged or punished in any way, not here, and certainly not in any sort of afterlife. I have had to learn to accommodate that, too. I have no choice, and expectation does not rule my thoughts and emotions some sixteen years after the fact. Emotional detachment is my goal. It's not easy, but then, most worthwhile things aren't.

I believe that as a biological organism, I have only one life to live. Therefore, I must endeavor to live in the present. This sky, this earth, this love, this joy, this sensation . . . in every blade of grass, life reminds me that this is all I have, and that I must be ever mindful of that knowledge.

Myra

My belief is very much a source of comfort.

I see death as a phase of life as a human.

Austin

I believe an individual's spirit, or soul, lives on, as an individual.

Louise

I am not real sure, but I know that there are many things we as humans cannot understand; for example: snowflakes. I think there are many forces we cannot explain.

Connie

45

I believe that my husband is in heaven. I believe that we will see each other again and that he is at peace in his new world. I made sure the minister at the hospital came to pray with me for him.

I am not a church-going person, but I am spiritual. This is and has been a source of comfort for me.

Austin

 My belief is very much a source of comfort. I believe that after death one goes on to their next chosen plane of existence. I see death as a phase of life as a human—even violent death. I believe that before we are born we "chose" (as Spirit) what we will experience in the human form. I don't think that Spirit judges life experience. I think Spirit just wants to experience EVERYTHING. Therefore no experience in what we call life is bad or wrong as to Spirit. But to us we need judgments in order for society to work.

Louise

 I believe an individual's spirit, or soul, lives on, as an individual. I believe from my own three experiences with it that there can be spontaneous communication between the living and those who have passed on. I had an experience of my husband a month or so after his death—a light, energy, and a sense of love. A few months later he came to me in a detailed dream full of sound, color, and feeling with some personal symbols . . . telling me he would always love me and it was OK to go on with my life. I can still bring up the visual scene, and the feeling of that dream. It is still comforting. When I stop and allow it, I can call up the feeling of being loved from many who have loved me, passed on, and send me love.

I believe when the time is right, souls can will be reincarnated to another human life on Earth to learn things they didn't learn during previous lifetimes. We always get a chance to get things right, to play the music of life correctly.

Connie

I am not real sure, but I know that there are many things we as humans cannot understand; for example: snowflakes. I think there are many forces we cannot explain. I fully support whatever anyone else comes up with that makes sense to them as long as it doesn't cause them or others more damage. It is also practical to me and comforting to know that I will continue in some way. I may be part of a tree or animal or another human as well. I don't know and I believe we don't know. I am comforted in knowing that I will, and my sister continues.

Now it is time to listen to Step Two of your audio component, or you may read the text that follows. You may download an audio version at http://svlp.org/resources.html.

Step Two Closing Exercise

To get ready for this experience, sit in a comfortable chair in a quiet place where you will not be interrupted ... then place your feet flat on the floor. ... Sit forward and lean back with your shoulders resting on the back of your chair. You may discover that you are sitting in a slant with your buttocks closer to the edge of your chair leaning back. (You may also lie down to do this.)

Place your hands on the upper part of your chest ... gently, one on top of the other ... and begin first by just noticing ... the weight of your hands resting on your chest. ... Make sure that your arms are not resting on the arms of the chair to get the full feel of the weight of your hands on your chest. ... Now ... notice the slight movement of your hands from your own breathing. ...

You may find that closing your eyes helps you to focus more on these slight sensations. Again ... notice the slight movement of your hands from your own breathing. ... You may also notice your heartbeat. ... Just notice this for a few moments. ... Make sure that your elbows are not resting on the chair, that they are free. ... Notice, again, the weight of your hands on your chest ... resting gently. Notice the rise and fall of your chest from your own breathing.

Now ... take a deep breath in through your nose and **hold it** *............ for as long as you can ... and when you are ready ... form your mouth into an O ... and slowly breath out ... let that air go ... all the way out. ... Then relax ... and ... slump ... keeping your hands in place ... just slump ... like a rag doll ... letting those muscles go ... and relax ... notice how well that chair is supporting you ... with nothing you need to do ... no place to go ... you can just to let go ... and relax.*

It is important NOT to do these deep breaths one right after the other. You may experience dizziness if you do. Do normal breathing in between the deep breaths.

Take another deep breath and hold it for as long as you can, and then ... form your mouth into an O ... and slowly breath out ... let that air go ... all the way out. ... Then relax ... and ... slump ... keeping your hands in place ... just slump ... like a rag doll ... letting those muscles go ... and relax. ...

The lungs are the most efficient eliminators of toxins in the body. The air we breathe in has impurities in it and our lungs filter this air. When we breathe out, we get rid of those toxins; we don't need them anymore.

Take another deep breath and hold it for as long as you can, and then ... form your mouth into an O ... and slowly breath out ... let that air go ... all the way out. ... Then relax ... and ... slump ... keeping your hands in place ... just slump ... like a rag doll ... letting those muscles go ... and relax. ...

The out breath is also the ... sigh ... the relaxation response. The out breath gets rid of some of the stress we feel as well as getting rid of the toxins filtered by our lungs. ...

Take one more deep breath and hold it for as long as you can, and then . . . form your mouth into an O . . . and slowly breath out . . . let that air go . . . all the way out. . . . Then relax . . . and . . . slump . . . keeping your hands in place . . . just slump . . . like a rag doll . . . letting those muscles go . . . and relax. . . .

To improve and practice the power of breathing . . . practice by taking deep breaths in and holding it for as long as you can in and out of your day. One at a time, with normal breaths in between deep breaths.

Take your time to notice being in the room . . . to your day . . . knowing you have strengthened your ability to feel lighter and perhaps calmer or a few moments of your day. . . .

Changes and Prevailing

How are you doing so far with the Journey you are taking in this workbook?

We have asked you to take account of who is there to support you.

The next path on your Journey with us is to acknowledge the changes that have occurred and ways that you are managing. How have you changed since the loss of your loved one? (Consider Physical, Emotional, Spiritual, Economic, Social, and Family Changes) You may have many competing priorities going on with the demands regarding the loss of your loved one.

Refer to the handout at the end of this section. Many survivors say they have had changes in all the areas of the handout. Ronnie Janoff-Bullman, in her book Shattered Assumptions, notes that the following beliefs may be shattered following trauma:

> The World Is Safe
> Life Has Meaning
> I Have Worth

This traumatic event has changed you and those around you. You won't go back to the way things were before. This loss is part of the quilt of who you are forever. This loss is part of your template, your Journey. You have choices to make that you would not have faced if you hadn't lost someone in a violent way.

Some people move out of their homes, change jobs, and change careers. You may be reviewing relationships and how they feel to you now. Some of the old ways don't fit and you will be seeking new ones.

We ask you to look at the Changes that may be occurring. Changes can include health, work, creativity, finances, exercise, routines, friends, and relationships, as well as a sense of pleasure. Changes are often painful, but some may improve

Three interventions guide the Restorative Retelling Model and are based on our natural abilities. They include:

- The ability to calm or quiet ourselves down.
- The ability to see ourselves as separate from others.
- The ability to be hopeful.

49

your life. You may notice a "dark" gift that in some way is a surprise outcome. Look at the three ways that our innate or natural abilities can be called upon to help. These are listed in the sidebar on the previous page. For additional reading, see The "Changed Forever" on page 174.

STEP THREE, QUESTION ONE

How have you Changed? Use the two following lists, "How Have You Changed?" and "How Have You Prevailed?" as guides and mark the changes that are most evident for you. Feel free to add some of your own, as we fully recognize everyone has differences.

HOW HAVE YOU CHANGED?

As you look through the following list, consider how you've changed since the person you loved died.

1. Physically
   —Weight gain/loss
   —Headaches
   —Sleep less/more
   —Stomach problems
   —Heart problems
   —Increased/decreased energy
   —Frequent accidents
   —Alcohol/drug abuse
   —High blood pressure
   —Forget to eat/overeat

2. Emotionally
   —Surges of grief
   —Trouble concentrating
   —Increased alone time
   —Difficulty being alone
   —Closer to loved ones
   —No interests
   —Forgetful
   —Rages/increased anger
   —Feel unsafe
   —Surprising strengths

3. Productivity: Work/School
   —Work excessively
   —Miss deadlines
   —Boss/coworker pressure
   —Lengthy blank stares
   —Unable to work
   —Employer is supportive

4. Financial
   —Unexpected costs worrisome
   —Help received from donations
   —Behind in bill paying
   —Don't care

5. Spiritually
   —Reconnecting with spiritual roots
   —Unsure what matters
   —No joy or pleasure
   —Meaninglessness
   —Feel disconnected
   —Increased spiritual awareness

6. Family/Relationships
   —Family rifts deepened
   —Increased family longing
   —Worried about family members
   —Mate doesn't understand

On this page, write the highlights of what you have discovered about the changes that have occurred.

What other changes would you add to this list?

How Have You Prevailed?

As you look through the following list, consider how you have prevailed since the person you loved died. Resiliencies listed here are from the contributions of leaders in the field. You may write responses on the blank lines, or circle the ones that apply to you.

1. Ted Rynearson (Violent Death Bereavement Society—VDBS.com)
   Pacification Strategies—the ways the you calm yourself, quiet yourself:

   _____

   _____

   Partitioning Strategies—how you describe your loved one's life interest as different from others: _____

   _____

   Perspective Strategies—the missions or memorials that come to mind to honor your loved one: _____

   _____

2. Shirley Murphy (University of Washington, Seattle)
   Caretaking of others: _____
   Faith-based involvement: _____

3. Wolin & Wolin (Project Resilience.com)
   • Insight
   • Independence
   • Morality
   • Relationships
   • Creativity
   • Humor

4. Marilyn Amour—The intense pursuit of what matters (University of Texas, Austin)
   • Fighting for what is right.
   • Living in ways that gives our loved one's life a purpose.
   • Using experiences to benefit others.
   • Living deliberately in an effort to give positive value to the loss.

5. From Walsh (Family Resilience)
   • Working as a team.
   • Creating rituals to honor loved one.
   • Creating a system to keep in touch with each other.

What other resiliencies would you add?

Resiliency Resources and Restorative Retelling can be found in Appendix V.

Survivor Voices

STEP THREE, QUESTION ONE

Dee
The world became very unsafe and a fearful place. Trust became difficult. In 1984. I thought I would never stop crying. I cried daily for over a year. I was unable to work. I left my job, but I don't remember leaving it. Black out memory of how I was not coping. My family in Texas fragmented over a few years. Because the family felt that my sister, Tara's mother, may be indirectly involved, they (and I) would have little to do with her. My father lost his business. My parents divorced. My grandmother, who Tara had lived with when she was murdered, passed away. My husband and I divorced.

In 1999 many of these feelings returned. The difference was that I had more tools to deal with them, and I knew to ask for help and was willing to get professional help.

Elena
Everything changed for me. The day my brother died, something in my parents died with him, and they were no longer the people I had known before, so that relationship in essence died as well. I was now responsible for making all the decisions of his funeral and his estate, things I had never dealt with before, and my parents were too distraught for me to turn to for help, so I felt very isolated. I loved his son, and for the sake of a continued relationship with my nephew I had to interact often with his mother, who is a person whom I would rather have nothing to do and whom I felt had added great pain to my brother's life.

Holidays and special family gatherings from then on had an emptiness to them and were no longer the carefree celebrations we had enjoyed in the past.

Spiritually I reconnected with my faith. I sensed that the only reason I could get up in the morning and keep going forward was that I was being carried by something or someone much stronger

> *The world became very unsafe and a fearful place.*
>
> Dee

> *Everything changed for me. The day my brother died, something in my parents died with him.*
>
> *Spiritually I reconnected with my faith.*
>
> Elena

than myself. I had no strength deal with all the consequences of my brother's death on my own and know there was someone greater guiding me.

I had difficulty focusing and there were times when I would just break out in tears when someone said something that triggered a memory of the event or my brother. I was absentminded and constantly had bruises on my thighs and arms from bumping into furniture or corners of walls.

An unexpected gift from all this is that I grew much closer to my family, and we shared our sorrow very openly with each other, listened to each other. I became very aware that every time I saw any of them it could very well be the last, so I did not take any time or conversation with them for granted. In time the fear of losing them diminished, but what has remained is that I still enjoy any time I am with people I care about.

Marina

I lost my sense of control/command/mastery of the world around me. I felt I was no longer a part of the world. I had to fight to contain an overwhelming sense of rage, as it could have really resulted in an outburst that would have caused pain to others. For the most part, I was successful. It was largely self-preservation—I had enough on my plate, without creating more sorrow and pain for myself, and for my loved ones. I became more honest in my personal life and my work. I felt I'd gone through the worst already, so there was really nothing to lose. I became less tolerant of people with substance abuse problems, emotional problems, relationship troubles, or money troubles.

By this I mean that I could no longer tolerate being around people who chose to remain in the "whining victim" mode. They weren't processing their problems, and on more than one occasion I realized that being around them was truly deleterious to my sense of stability, health, and well-being.

So a lot of marginal relationships fell by the wayside.

> *I lost my sense of control/command/mastery of the world around me. I had to fight to contain an overwhelming sense of rage, as it could have really resulted in an outburst that would have caused pain to others. For the most part, I was successful.*
>
> Marina

> *I know that my life will never be the same. It has been a journey, and many days I would give everything to go back to my old life, but I know that is not possible, so I try to find the joy in my new life.*
>
> Myra

There were a few I was compelled to keep, so I took steps to limit my time with those folks, and to set clear boundaries.

What else? I had to force myself to be a part of the greater world, to socialize. I knew instinctively that it would help me combat my sense of numbness and apathy. On some level, I think I was trying to retrain myself how to live, like someone who experiences a devastating physical injury. I figured if I went through the motions enough times, the will to live and go on would somehow sink in eventually. I smiled a lot. Sometimes it felt pretty counterfeit and empty. Again, I determined that if I did it consistently, the smile would penetrate my psychic pain, do a U-turn, and some day come from deep inside. It finally did, but I think that is because I did the hard work in therapy, and in my daily life. Plus, I'm a monster of resiliency. I remember looking at myself in the mirror from the day I learned about the murder. My face was etched with profound sorrow, yet I smiled, and thought, "Look at you! You're still standing. You can still smile. What a monster, like Godzilla or King Kong! They can shoot you, bomb you, even take away your oxygen, but you just keep on going. You BOUNCE!"

It was strangely exhilarating. I used it for all it was worth.

Myra
I have changed a lot from the time of my husband's death. I was a confident person, sure of my future, and did not worry about how I was going to spend the remainder of my life. Now, I have had to make my own future and take care of myself. I lost a lot of weight; it was my way of controlling a world that seemed out of control for me. I have now gained most of that weight back and don't feel the need to have such control, as I know my future will be okay. I kept my job, I stayed in my home, and most of my friends have stayed the same. I know that my life will never be the same. I am constantly reminded of the places and things he taught me, yet I have to live for today. It has been a journey, and many days I would give everything to

The ways I have changed include a deeper sense of loss of loved ones in my family. The loss of my nephew has brought my family closer together.

Austin

It has made me more compassionate and understanding.

It has made me appreciate all the people who have made the effort and written books about life, love, spiritual growth, philosophy, etc. I am a constant reader and these authors have given me knowledge, strength, insight, inspiration, and support.

Louise

go back to my old life, but I know that is not possible, so I try to find the joy in my new life.

Austin

The ways I have changed include a deeper sense of loss of loved ones in my family. I suppose I am feeling more "sorry for myself" than before, thinking that I have an "undue" amount of loss of family members. Though this is in conflict with my spiritual belief as previously stated. I also feel a deeper connection to my only remaining immediate family member. The loss of my nephew has brought my family closer together.

Louise

I see myself as a strong person, capable of coping with what life brings. If I can come through that and accomplish what I have, then I must be OK. I feel I have more understanding of life and people than I would have otherwise had, or reached it earlier in life. It has made me more compassionate and understanding. I see myself as able to forgive. I feel I have been loved and (most of the time) feel loved.

It has given me a strong feeling of "It can happen to me," rather than a common belief that "It can't/won't happen to me." I don't dismiss possibilities and try to assess things, circumstances, relationships thoroughly before I make a decision or take chances (money, relationships, actions, etc.). I feel careful.

I wonder sometimes if it has made me less willing or able to totally commit myself with deep love to someone in another close relationship because I might lose this person, too. I've been willing to try, but three more marriages and two additional relationships of 4-5 years each haven't worked or been truly fulfilling. It is discouraging.

I don't feel close to very many people—they are acquaintances only. I don't feel "known" and am often lonely. Maybe it is just how/who I am, not related to his death. I often don't

> *I haven't been trying out for the Olympics, but I have indeed concentrated my efforts in this area (of violent death).*
>
> Connie

57

volunteer information about myself or my thoughts/ feelings to others unless they ask and seem interested. I create my own shell. A lot of people don't seem interested or like to talk about the same things I do. I really enjoy the few that do.

Many things in life add up to the above changes. One major one, inseparable from my personal experience with living through and after his death, has been my career working in mental health treatment facilities. Reading patients' records has made me aware of how many circumstances are present in people's lives; how much individuals cope with; how resilient people can be; how much receiving support can mean; how much difference reflection, honesty, and insight can make in bringing forth peace of mind and self-acceptance.

It has made me appreciate all the people who have made the effort and written books about life, love, spiritual growth, philosophy, etc. I am a constant reader and these authors have given me knowledge, strength, insight, inspiration, and support. Three that helped me in the early years after his death were Parent Effectiveness Training" (PET), I'm OK—You're OK, and the writing of Teilhard de Chardin.

Changes:

> *1. Physically—overeat sweets; my stomach is always the first thing to be affected when I am stressed.*

> *2. Emotionally—have many of these occasionally, but after all these years, I don't know that they relate to his death.*

> *3. Productivity—sometimes feel driven to "accomplish," make a contribution to the world; most likely related to my father's mandate: "it is the responsibility of those who have much to give back" or to feel worthy.*

> *4. Financial— [blank]*

> *5. Increased spiritual awareness; realizing spirituality, religion, and church are different.*

> *6. Family relationships—add one choice: Became closer over time.*

 ### Connie
I don't think change came for me for awhile, except for having a driving force to understand human behavior. I just wanted to know why people do what they do. Why does someone murder my sweet, innocent sister who had no mean bone in her body that any of us could find. The biggest change has come from my specialized work with violent death bereavement since 1997. My world was organized around shades of gray; today, I see a lot more black and white.

There really are some good and bad people and behaviors. I haven't been trying out for the Olympics, but I have indeed concentrated my efforts in this area (of violent death). So I have found that some folks don't find me much fun. What I have to talk about isn't what they want to hear about. I don't have to go see "The Passion of Christ" to get in touch with real suffering. I have, now, hundreds of real stories that get recalled daily. I am selective regarding what entertainment I watch on TV and at the movies. I go out of my way to make sure I do things that counterbalance my work with survivor families. I savor my alone time more than I ever did.

STEP THREE, QUESTION TWO

How have you managed? What are you doing, even for a moment, that has you away from what has happened, that gives you a break and helps you keep on going? What do you do to decrease the intense pain and chaos that accompanies your unnatural death? What have you found that keeps you from being absorbed and gives you a momentary break? Write here what you have experienced.

Survivor Voices

STEP THREE, QUESTION TWO

Dee
After Tara was murdered, I received a little pre-inheritance from my Grandmother. One of the things Bob and I did was to purchase a sailboat. We would sail. That is one thing we did together as a family. It was the best. I loved being on the water.

In 1999, I would get out of my head by beading—jewelry beading. I would go to the beach and to outings with friends. I also would do volunteer work through a self-help group and reach out to others.

Elena
In the beginning I had such strong and overwhelming feelings that the only thing that would help was to go in the church and just sit in the silence. I felt as if that was the only time I could actually breathe and find some escape.

Later, what helped me greatly was going for long walks alone and just looking at the beauty around me. I needed to be alone with my thoughts and try to grasp the reality of what had happened.

Eventually I did begin to cook again and that was a time I felt happy at creating something that others enjoyed. I like that while I am involved in cooking my mind is occupied and absorbed in something fun.

Marina
From the day I learned of Dad's murder, I made myself eat good, nutritious, delicious food. I treated myself to the best chocolates, veggies, fruits, and meats. I exercised like a madwoman, both running and weight training. It was almost as if I were trying to outrun the corrosive rage, hatred, terror, and grief. Often I

I would get out of my head by beading—jewelry beading. I would go to the beach and to outings with friends. I also would do volunteer work through a self-help group and reach out to others.

Dee

The only thing that would help was to go in the church and just sit in the silence.

Elena

I made myself eat good, nutritious, delicious food.

I made it a point to see the incredible beauty in the smallest of things. "Going macro" seemed to make more manageable a world I perceived as threatening.

Marina

60

ran to the point of exhaustion, which was a good thing—most of the time. I was lucky I didn't ever trip, or break something. It's a challenge to be mindful of one's physical safety at such a time.

In the spirit of Buddhism, I made it a point to see the incredible beauty in the smallest of things. "Going macro" seemed to make more manageable a world I perceived as threatening. My dad lived in a resort town about two hours' drive from where I live, so I stayed in a hotel near his house. What a sense of unreality! It was Fourth of July weekend, and families celebrated all around me as I strolled the hotel grounds with my boyfriend. We went to the poolside bar/restaurant. It was nighttime. I was out of it. Such profound agony. Then I heard a quacking noise. The ducks that frequented a nearby pond were wandering under the tables unconcernedly, cadging food from the diners. I forced myself to meditate briefly upon the beautiful patterns created by the feathers on the wings of one duck. What wondrous complexity! Plus, I love birds, and I think that there is something inherently whimsical about ducks, with their funny quacks and waddling gait. Their squabbles. The whole package. For one brief moment I was suffused with a sense of nature's beauty. I wanted to cry for the joy of it, instead of crying for my dad. It actually worked for a short while—enough to make me see that here was an open door, a pathway toward the life I had lost.

I also went to Dog Beach to watch the dogs caper in the surf and sand. Hiking in the mountains or walking on the beach reminded me that I was an infinitesimal part of a universe that has existed for billions of years. I made myself remember that the world would go on without me from the moment of my death, and that I had to live the precious time I had left.

Continuing my work as a volunteer child abuse case assessor took me out of my own situation so that I could focus on those who were far worse off than I was. It made me grateful for my childhood, difficult as it was. Reading about the helplessness of the innocent really brought home that I was a powerful, capable adult person who had the privilege of making her own choices.

The world breaks everyone and afterward many are strong at the broken places.
Ernest Hemingway

I was saddened by Robin Williams' suicide. I never thought about suicide as self murder.... I feel for those left behind.

My aunt was never the same after my cousin's suicide. She applauded our efforts on The Journey workbook. She said she wished she'd gone through therapy. She thought her life would have been a little better if she had.
Marina

Where there is life, there is hope.
Stephen Hawking

I tried really hard to see things as they were, not as I wanted them to be. This became my "mantra," if you will.

I went back to the scene of the murder, and the town where my dad lived, many times. By that time I was in therapy, and I was aware that I was experiencing what is called "seeking and yearning" behavior. Pure compulsion. But it was also part of a conscious effort to walk right into and through that which I feared the most, thus desensitizing myself over time. Maybe it wouldn't work for everyone, but facing my worst fears was ultimately an enriching experience. I also looked at pictures of my dad's life. I held, smelled, and studied his belongings. I danced and sang: sad songs, happy songs, reflective songs, dancing songs. I cried and cried, chuckled, screamed with rage, terror, and disbelief. No one could hear me. This was a good thing. I was free to do whatever. Music and lyrics helped me to process and digest the truly indigestible.

It took a long, long, time.

Myra

It was a long journey; the first two years were horrible. I was a mess emotionally. I thought I was doing okay, but later found that I had stuffed all of my bills into a drawer for a whole year!! My therapist helped me a lot. I cut out the sugar (which adds to the emotional rollercoaster); I redid my house one room at a time; I spent time with my friends and made a plan for every bit of free time. I followed all of the suggestions from Hospice. I found new interests and made sure I spoke to my friends about their lives every week. I made sure my holidays were different. I got rid of all of the Christmas ornaments from our lives together and bought all new ones. I changed all of my holiday traditions, changed the pictures in my house, and finally could spend time in the garage where my husband shot himself. I listened to new music and carried makeup with me always because when the wave of grief hit I would have a repair kit. This rarely happens now, but for the first three years it was almost every day.

Austin

Prevailing is no problem. My faith in Spirit gives me support, and I feel that my Nephew has moved on to another plane where he belongs. I feel that his death is a "learning" process for those in his family. I don't really believe that we need to "learn" anything, but it appears so in the way we humans process in life.

I never felt intense pain and chaos. There was certainly stress and pain for my family, and I supported them with strength and support without getting into their chaos and pain. I think my dedication to their needs helped shield me from what they were going through.

In my mind it is OK and natural to go through "chaos and pain," but I can be of more assistance to others if I am not involved in it. As stated above, I do feel a sense of loss, but the "loss" of Brad, I feel, is part of his life's plan that he chose before being born.

Louise

Taking care of my children was my main impetus for life, for staying alive, just after my husband's death. I had a strong desire to raise them MY way and not leave their upbringing to my mother or sister.

My first major decision in managing my life was to go back to college and finish my degree. I wanted to be able to get a well-paying job to support my children.

I made conscious decisions not to live in fear. To live fully, to not become mired in "what if?" and "whose fault was it?" questions; to not succumb to "Poor me" attitudes; to do the best I could as a parent but still take care of my Self. I still maintain those decisions.

I invested the financial settlement that went to my children to pay for their going to college.

For several years after getting remarried and then divorced, I decided on a family hobby of hot-air ballooning. I bought a hot-air balloon in partnership with two other owners and got a pilot's license, both my son and daughter crewed and flew. We went to rallies, did demonstrations at school and work, met many other friendly people.

I keep intellectually occupied, continually educating myself by taking classes, reading, etc. I keep busy following new interests. It is an effort to keep social.

I make an effort to stay spiritually attuned and try to live up to my overall life goal: to be a loving person.

I keep reminding myself of all the many things I have to be thankful for.

Making Sense Meditation

A play on words: "making sense of your world through your senses."

Smell: the air right before and after it rains; baking bread and cookies; the roses in my yard.

Taking care of my children was my main impetus for life, for staying alive, just after my husband's death.

I made conscious decisions not to live in fear. To live fully, to not become mired in "what if?" and "whose fault was it?" questions; to not succumb to "poor me" attitudes; to do the best I could as a parent but still take care of my Self.

Louise

Sound: the water feature in my yard—trickling water.

Some specific music: songs and lyrics:

> *"How Great Thou Art," Jim Neighbors*
>
> *"Have You Ever Been Mellow," Olivia Newton-John*
>
> *"The Rose," Bette Midler*
>
> *"Love Changes Everything," Andrew Lloyd Weber (in "Aspects of Love")*
>
> *Some of the earthy country—western ballads*
>
> *"El Paso," Marty Robbins*
>
> *"I Walk the Line," Johnny Cash*
>
> *"I Just Want to Dance With You," George Strait*

Taste: some chocolate candies; raspberries & grapefruit (with sugar).

Touch: I miss it very much.

Seeing: Long views: views of mountains, the ocean, the desert; my granddaughter's innocent face.

Connie

When I answer this question, I need to talk more about today than in 1961 to say how I have managed. I realize that I, like so many others that work with violent death, we are changed forever, too. (Read The "Forever Changed" in Appendix III.) That is true for those of us who have had a violent loss, and it is also true for those who work with this area. Not realizing the impact when I was first working with this program that I helped set up, I found myself, one night, stopped at a four-way stop sign waiting for the light to turn green. Of course, it didn't, and eventually I came out of this stunned state. Thank goodness there was no traffic. I know it has been harder for me to be compassionate with people who haven't helped much to give this program firm and stable roots. And there has been more than one person to acknowledge my impatience and expectations. I have been quite unwavering, though, in my persistence in providing services to those who have lost someone to homicide or other violent deaths. And, every time I hear another story, I am so convinced that what we are doing is indeed very important and also helpful work. We truly are helping folks regain their lives and live better with what has happened to them.

Now it is time to listen to Step Three of the audio component, or you may read the text that follows. You may download an audio version at http://svlp.org/resources.html.

Step Three Closing Exercise

Again . . . to get ready for this experience, sit in a comfortable chair in a quiet place where you will not be interrupted . . . then place your feet flat on the floor. . . . Sit forward and lean back with your shoulders resting on the back of your chair.

Place your hands on the upper part of your chest . . . gently, one on top of the other . . . and begin first by just noticing . . . the weight of your hands resting on your chest. . . . Make sure that your arms are not resting on the arms of the chair to get the full feel of the weight of your hands on your chest. . . . Now . . . notice the slight movement of your hands from your own breathing. . . .

You may find that closing your eyes helps you to focus more on these slight sensations. Again . . . notice the slight movement of your hands from your own breathing. . . . You may also notice your heartbeat. . . . Just notice this for a few moments. . . . Make sure that your elbows are not resting on the chair, that they are free. . . . Notice, again, the weight of your hands on your chest . . . resting gently. Notice the rise and fall of your chest from your own breathing.

*Now . . . take a deep breath in through your nose and **hold it** . . . . for as long as you can . . . and when you are ready . . . form your mouth into an O . . . and slowly breath out . . . let that air go . . . all the way out. . . . Then relax . . . and . . . slump . . . keeping your hands in place . . . just slump . . . like a rag doll . . . letting those muscles go . . . and relax . . . notice how well that chair is supporting you . . . with nothing you need to do . . . no place to go . . . you can just to let go . . . and relax.*

Making Sense

This is a time when so much does not make sense . . . but one thing we do know is that when you take this kind of time out ... to take in one deep breath and hold it . . . and then slowly let it go . . . it makes sense in giving you increased calm, amid so much that doesn't make sense . . . and while you take this kind of time out . . . that is . . . take in a nice deep breath and hold it . . . and slowly let it go . . . you may also make sense out of something that is a favorite smell . . . something that you remember or can imagine that you enjoy . . . what might that be? You may want to stay with what first smell that comes up in your mind . . . as that might be most significant . . . a favorite smell . . . something that you enjoy . . . mine is a gardenia . . . and I have been known to smell it long after it has turned brown. . . . What is your favorite smell? . . . Enjoy it for a moment or two longer . . . mmmmmmmm.

Another sense that you may have enjoyed is sound . . . what is a favorite sound of yours? Perhaps some music . . . the sound of a waterfall . . . a particular bird . . . children laughing . . . what is a sound you enjoy . . . or what sound is pleasurable to you? Enjoy your sound for a moment or two while you remind yourself to take another deep breath and hold it . . . and slowly let it go. . . .

Now think of a favorite taste . . . perhaps it is something you haven't enjoyed for awhile . . . what is a favorite taste? . . . mmmmmmmm. One that I usually think of is lobster . . . a favorite from being raised in New England. What is a favorite taste for you? Enjoy that memory and see if you can taste it now . . . enjoy your favorite taste for another moment of two. Very good. . . .

Another sense that may make sense in this time . . . when so much does not make sense is . . . the sense of touch. What do you love to touch? Perhaps the feel of leather . . . soft fur, the skin of someone you love . . . what you enjoy touching . . . enjoy that for a moment or two . . . and take in another deep breath . . . hold it . . . then slowly let it go. . . .

In taking this kind of time to focus . . . to pay attention to things that make sense . . . that can give you some quiet . . . some soothing . . . think of something you like seeing ... something that pulls your attention . . . could it be a waterfall . . . trees full of bloom in the spring time . . . how you looked dressed for prom . . . or a mountain lake like the one I saw when I drove through Aspen. . . . What do you enjoy seeing?

Taking moments out like this may help you live better with what has happened . . . little moments of quiet . . . calm . . . sensory focus can help quiet and buffer the mind. . . .

To improve and practice the power of breathing, practice by taking deep breaths in and holding them for as long as you can, in and out of your day. One at a time, with normal breaths in between deep breaths. And pay more attention to your senses, one at a time.

Take whatever time you need to refocus on your day . . . slowly opening your ideas, and begin you next activity.

Complications

STEP FOUR, QUESTION ONE

Do you have any special dates coming up? Birthdays? Anniversaries? Holidays?

List them here.

_____

_____

_____

_____

_____

Let others know when these dates come up to obtain more support. Think of an activity that will have you remember your loved one during those anniversary times.

An area we would like to cover in this section is to talk about events that were already happening when this loss occurred; examples include: upcoming marriage, a family member being treated for cancer, a new job, or someone who has a problem with alcohol. Many accompanying circumstances and complications may intensify matters for you.

Areas that may prompt you to ask for extra help from a professional are depression, post-traumatic stress, and substance abuse, as well as family discord.

Depression—such as lack of concentration or focus, inability to make decisions, feelings of worthlessness, hopelessness, loss of identity, social isolation, weight loss or gain, feeling suicidal or homicidal, intense emotional swings, inability to attend work school, sleep problems, lack of pleasure and meaning.

High level of symptoms that meet criteria for acute stress disorder could be prevented from developing into a more prolonged disorder of PTSD in many instances if treatment is provided early.

Bryant, 2003

Shirley Murphy Study

A sample of 171 mothers and fathers from Medical Examiner records were followed for two years. Thirty-six percent still met case criteria for PTSD two years after the death of a [12- to 28-year-old] child.

Medical authorities first accepted PTSD as a psychiatric condition in 1980 at the urging of Vietnam Vets.

Veterans with PTSD are more likely to have heart attacks years later. This new study is the first to link PTSD with health problems 10-15 years later.

Laura Kubzansky
Harvard, 2007

Post-traumatic stress—includes panic attacks, flashbacks, replaying and reliving what happened, nightmares, terror, intrusive thoughts and images.

Substance Abuse—excessive use of drugs or alcohol. This may be used as a form of self-medication and may need intervention and/or medically prescribed treatments and protocols.

Life events can also complicate and add to your stress: new job, marriage, baby, live a long way away from place of loss, family rivalries, and financial strain.

Grief: A Normal and Natural Response to Loss

Review the lists of symptoms that may be occurring. This first list has been compiled by Survivors from both Orange County and San Diego County in California. Circle the ones that you are experiencing.

MOST PEOPLE WHO SUFFER A LOSS EXPERIENCE ONE OR MORE OF THE FOLLOWING:

- Feel tightness in the throat or heaviness in the chest.
- Feel thumping, erratic beats in the heart. Very aware of heart actions.
- Have an empty feeling in their stomach and loss (or gain) of appetite or nausea.
- Feel restless and look for activity, but have difficulty concentrating.
- Feel in a trance, want to just sit and stare.
- Feel as though the loss isn't real, that it didn't actually happen. (This may include trying to find the loved one.)
- Feel light-headed and dizzy a lot.
- Sense the loved one's presence (this may include expecting the person to walk in the door at the usual time, or hearing his/her voice, or seeing his/her face).
- Have headaches frequently.
- Wander aimlessly, forget, and don't finish things they've started to do around the house.
- Have difficulty sleeping, and have dreams or visions of their loved one frequently.
- Feel guilty or angry over things that happened or didn't happen in the relationship.

THESE ARE ALL NORMAL GRIEF RESPONSES.

YOU MAY ALSO EXPERIENCE:

DISBELIEF
You expect to wake up any minute from this nightmare. It can't be true. You can't cry, because you don't believe it.

SHOCK
Nature's Shock Absorbers work to soften the blow by putting you temporarily in a state of shock. You feel numb and dazed. Your emotions are frozen. You go through the motions, like a robot.

CRYING
Deep emotions suddenly well up, seeking release as loud sobbing and crying. Give yourself time for tears. They can help.

PHYSICAL SYMPTOMS
You may sleep or eat too little or too much. You may have physical aches, pains, numbness, or weakness. Check with a doctor to rule out other causes. Usually the symptoms fade gradually.

DENIAL
You know the fact of death, but you forget. You expect your loved one to telephone or walk in the door. You expect to wake up from a nightmare.

"WHY" QUESTIONS
"Why did he/she have to die?" You don't expect an answer, but you need to ask repeatedly.

REPEATING
Over and over again, you tell the same story, think the same thoughts. Repeating helps absorb the reality, or result in getting stuck.

SELF-CONTROL
You control your emotions to fulfill your responsibilities or to rest from the pain. Self-control can shape and give rhythm to your grieving, but constant, rigid self-control can block healing.

REALITY
"It really happened." You feel as if you're getting worse. Actually, reality has just hit, and support from friends and family may be diminishing.

CONFUSION
You can't think. You forget in mid-sentence. You are disorganized and impatient.

IDEALIZING
You remember only good traits, as if your loved one was perfect. You find it hard to accept the not-so-perfect living. Your loved one's idiosyncrasies or imperfect traits become endearing reminders of her or him.

IDENTIFYING
Wanting to stay close, you copy your loved one's style of dress, hobbies, interests, or habits. You may carry a special object of his or hers.

ENVY
You envy others. Their pleasure with their loved ones makes you realize keenly what you have lost.

FRUSTRATION
Your life path has changed and you are not sure where you will go next. You think you're not coping with grief "right."

BITTERNESS

Temporary feelings of resentment and hatred, especially toward those in some way responsible for your loss, are natural. This may help you steer toward those you have more trust for, but habitual bitterness can drain energy and block healing.

WAITING

The struggle is over, but your zest has not returned. You are in limbo, exhausted, and life seems flat.

HOPE

You believe you will get better. The good days out balance the bad. Sometimes you can work effectively, enjoy activities, and really care for others.

MISSING

You never stop missing your loved one. Particular days, places, and activities can bring back the pain as intensely as ever.

COMMITMENT

You know you have a choice. Life won't be the same, but you decide to actively begin building a new life.

SEEKING

You take initiative, renewing your involvement with former friends and try new activities.

HANGING ON

Some days you hang on to the grief, which is familiar. Letting go is more of a final good-bye to your loved one. You let go gradually.

PEACE

You can reminisce about your loved one with a sense of peace. You're able to face your own future.

LIFE OPENS UP

Life has value and meaning again. You can enjoy, appreciate, and anticipate events. You are willing to let the rest of your life be all it can be.

Unanswerable Whys . . .

You may be asking lots of "Whys?" Circle the words listed below that describe what you are experiencing.

Numbing

I feel like a zombie; I don't care about anything.

Flashbacks

I felt like it was happening all over again!

Obsessive Retelling

Remaining possessed and "stuck" in this morbid retelling of a loved one's death for months or years.

The Dying Narrative
The Dying Narrative
The Dying Narrative
The Dying Narrative

Anger/Rage

How could this happen? How could he do this?

Compulsive Questioning Behavior

The need to know every detail of the circumstances surrounding the traumatic event; includes multiple investigative and record-keeping activities.

Trying to regain control of that which is out of control. The belief is that the more the event is understood, the more the survivor has a sense of control and prevention of future harm.

I must know every single detail about what happened!

When someone dies, it is natural to mourn their loss—to think of them with sorrow and miss their presence in your life.... If they died from a natural death (from disease or old age), then the dying would be understandable. This is not the case with unnatural dying; when someone close dies an unnatural death, you not only mourn their loss but are forced to adjust to the unnatural way that they died.

E.K. Rynearson, MD,
Retelling Violent Death

In *All the Wrong Places: A Life Lost and Found,* author Philip Connors describes the impact of his brother's suicide on own his life:

My mistake, I belatedly realized, was to fixate on his death that I lost contact with who he'd been in life.

I could count on one hand the number of times I'd found someone willing to talk about him for longer than a minute or two in the six years since his death.

Weathering the Storm

Hyper-vigilance

Being hyper alert, jumpy, or skittish. Soldiers report this experience when returning home, as do violent death survivors, who frequently scan their environment for danger.

I am constantly on guard, scanning my surroundings for threats.

Hyper-startle Response

Involuntary, exaggerated surprise reactions to triggering sights and sounds resulting in physical startle reactions such as jumpiness or screaming; related to hyper-vigilance.

I keep jumping out of my skin!

Avoidance

Efforts to distract and deflect thoughts of traumatic loss; may cause sleep disruption; for example, persistently working overtime, cleaning, studying.

I don't want to think about it; I don't like to talk about it. If I just keep busy!

Guilt

If only . . . I could have prevented this!

I am sure there is something I could have done.

Survivor Voices

STEP FOUR, QUESTION ONE

Dee

I experienced so many things on the list. I was in shock. When I was told what had happened, the words were inconceivable to me—they would not compute. Bob had to shout them to me. The tightness in my throat and chest lasted forever, it seemed. The disbelief. I received a Christmas card in the mail 3 days after she had died. She had mailed it the day she died. For an instant it felt like it had not happened at all. I even felt joy. But only for an instant.

When I traveled home over the next few years, I did feel like she would walk through the door at any moment or I could walk into her bedroom and she would be there playing her guitar. I was angry that Tara worked so hard to better her life only to have it end like this. She had a very difficult childhood and was determined to be a success—a doctor. I wondered WHY she had to die. She was so careful. She knew personal danger from other's experiences.

Elena

The symptom that was most profound for me when I heard of my brother's death was a sudden coldness and emptiness. I felt this in my chest and a longing ache in my arms. I felt as if someone had carved the Grand Canyon into my soul. I began to sob uncontrollably and it was so intense that at the same time I was stunned that such intense emotion was coming out of me.

For the longest time I would be triggered and start crying at comments that normally would have made me laugh or think or not even react. It was as if the only response within me was intense uncontrollable anguish.

I had nightmares, too, of either looking for my brother and not finding him or that I was being chased by something terrible that wanted to kill me and was moving very fast while I could only

I experienced so many things on the list. I was in shock. When I was told what had happened, the words were inconceivable to me—they would not compute.

I was angry that Tara worked so hard to better her life only to have it end like this.

Dee

I felt as if someone had carved the Grand Canyon into my soul.

For the longest time I would be triggered and start crying.

Elena

73

run as if in deep thick mud. I would wake up terrified and covered in sweat, my chest pounding. I was afraid that these symptoms would never pass but they slowly diminished over time; others, however, arose.

As time went on, I had more and more anger with my brother that he had died and left the mess of his life for me to deal with. I felt it especially strong when I had to interact with his ex-wife for the sake of a relationship with my nephew. I also blamed him because my mother had finally gone into remission from breast cancer just before his death. Within two months of his death the cancer returned. I knew it was the stress of his death that contributed to its return. This was very confusing for me because I also missed him and was trying to understand how he could take his own life.

In time and through great friends, my faith journey and very importantly this support process as well, I have come to a place of peace which I never thought would be possible. I can understand that my brother suffered greatly and was trying to stop the pain. I can remember him again with love and even laugh at the many great memories we had together. My life has great meaning and purpose, and I live much more deliberately than I ever did before his death.

Marina

My dad's birthday, April 17th, is still a very important anniversary for me. I actually forgot about it this past year. I didn't remember until a day or two after the fact. After eight years, it felt kind of good to forget—to have some distance from the date, and from what it has always meant to me.

The last days I saw him alive, June 16th and 17th, were very important to me. That lasted three or four years.

The day he was murdered, July 1, was important for about five years afterward. These latter two have faded in importance as well. It's a relief. I am too vibrant a person to carry that heavy burden forever. Gone is gone.

People don't really know what to say, and they don't want to bring it up and remind you if you aren't already thinking about it.

Louise

Mom was catatonic, in a frozen state. I don't remember how long that was, but I know she didn't eat and her eyes were empty. Dad, who had a history of alcohol problems, drank more; he blamed himself for not giving my sister a ride that morning.

Connie

Austin

I do not suffer from any of the symptoms listed.

Louise

I always remember, pause and think about it on August 9th. I guess no one else remembers, or at least they don't mention it unless I do. People don't really know what to say, and they don't want to bring it up and remind you if you aren't already thinking about it.

Connie

The life events that were occurring at and after the time were the following:

I had just gotten married. My mom, my new husband's mom, and I took my husband to the airport to catch a flight for his new duty station. I was to follow him as soon as he found a place for us. On the way there, the radio had reported a girl had been murdered in our town. This was something that never happened in our small, New England town. I guessed it was a "wild" girl in my High School class.

At the airport, an announcement came over the loudspeaker for my older sister's maiden name. None of us responded to that call as she was married, in Florida, and had a different last name. On the way home from the airport, they announced the name of my younger sister as the murder victim. My mother stopped the car.

I don't know how we got to the police station, nor how we got home again. Today, they do not announce the victim's name until the next of kin have been notified. Once home, Mom was catatonic, in a frozen state. I don't remember how long that was, but I know she didn't even eat and her eyes were empty. Dad, who had a history of alcohol problems, drank more; he blamed himself for not giving my sister a ride when he saw her that morning that she died. He told me years later that his drinking almost caused his death several times.

Since my wedding had just happened, we had a lot of great and recent photos of Tiny. My brother had just had a fight with her and told her he wished that she was dead. He never forgave himself for that and punished himself with poor self-care and died young.

I realize as I tell the story how I view it, everyone in my family would tell a different version, their version. In all families, what matters is each person's story that belongs to them. What they remember, what they observed, and what they experienced.

This page intentionally left blank. You are encouraged to use it for writing your story or keeping notes.

STEP FOUR, QUESTION TWO

What are you experiencing? As we mentioned before, this workbook is not a replacement for professional services. You were not meant to deal with this alone.

We don't get over it.
Deborah Spungen

Research shows that these consuming thoughts and images put one at greater risk for health-related problems:

Reenactment

Revenge

Rescue

Remorse

Reunion

Rynearson, 1997

Life events that are complicating my situation are:

Survivor Voices

STEP FOUR, QUESTION TWO

Dee

In 1984, I would take a soak bath. I tried to ask questions to find out what really happened. I would let myself cry. I would take my kids ice skating or to the library or the zoo. In 1999, when it all was returned to me, I embraced relaxing techniques I had learned to calm myself. I listened to music. Read. Walked.

Elena

I made a deliberate choice to not ignore the feelings I was experiencing and to allow them to speak to me and bring me healing. It was very important to me to have a person to speak with about how my brother's death had touched every aspect of my life and to allow me to vent all the anger associated with that.

Marina

It was weird at the beginning. I felt as if I had been carved up by a cruel knife. It was as if huge chunks of fat and muscle had been chopped away, leaving only essential bone and sinew—the bare minimum necessary to keep me moving. I had terrible headaches. I felt like someone had opened up my abdomen in order to pull out my entrails and drag me around by them. Inside-out. Hot and cold. Brain like cold cement, gut like molten lava.

It was the death of my illusions. Ideas of right and wrong were turned upside down. Even today, expressions like, "Good things come to good people, "It's meant to be" and "It's karma" make my lip curl in bitter cynicism. I have to take care to keep my mouth shut when others say these things. The murder and its aftermath marked the death of magical thinking on my part. I leave that to the innocents now.

It was weird at the beginning. I felt as if I had been carved up by a cruel knife. . . . I had trouble concentrating. It was almost impossible to read even a paragraph.

Marina

The Difficult Climb

What else? I was very aware of my heart actions. I often wondered if my heart would just give out at some point.

My digestion was somewhat dodgy. There was definitely some irregularity. I suffered from insomnia, which had never been a problem before. It is a problem which lingers in lesser form today, mostly when I am experiencing either situational or free-floating anxiety. Breathing exercises and visualization help with that to some degree.

I experienced weight loss in spite of a hearty appetite. It must have been the frequent adrenaline dumps. Oftentimes I would feel thirsty, spent, or exhausted. It was the kind of exhaustion I couldn't sleep away. I would wake up exhausted, and think, "Oh, no. The murder hasn't gone away. It's still real, all of it, like a 50-lb. anvil I can't shove off my chest, damn it." My blood pressure increased. That alarmed me AND pissed me off, as I have always worked hard to maintain the blood pressure and resting heart rate of an athlete.

I had trouble concentrating. It was almost impossible to read even a paragraph, which really interfered with my work. Forget about reading the news. Forget about reading for pleasure or distraction. That was all gone. Just like that.

I felt surges of grief, rage, frustration, and impotence, and embarrassment at not being able to control these unruly emotions. I felt unsafe. It was as if danger lurked around every corner. Logically, I knew this was not the case, but it didn't matter, because emotion and instinct overtook logic.

I was forgetful. To this day, forgetfulness is a problem. There has been some improvement, but it takes a lot of effort. It's as if some nasty, slobbering, dark thing reached into my brain and tore out a chunk of it. After sixteen years, I think it's safe to say that it ain't coming back. Thanks, you murdering Bitch.

Spiritually, I felt a sense of utter meaninglessness. Before the trial, I clung mightily to the belief

> *On the plus side, I realized how strong I was. I told myself that I was a warrior. I told myself that a warrior had to stay strong for battle, so I took really good care of myself.*
>
> Marina

79

that justice would be served. That kept me going. After we lost the trial, I felt a sense of total nihilism. Nothing meant anything. All previous beliefs were incinerated. I was a pile of ashes. I was bitter—disconnected totally from my previous life. I felt like an outlaw. I started having panic attacks. Thank goodness my boyfriend had experienced them years before, and told me that no, I wasn't dying. I read about them on WebMD, and was able to teach myself to separate reality from imagination, and to breathe. I haven't had one for years now.

On the plus side, I realized how strong I was. I told myself that I was a warrior. I told myself that a warrior had to stay strong for battle, so I took really good care of myself. In spite of the unruly emotions, I felt very powerful. It seemed I was imbued with a meta-knowledge about life and its workings. I sensed that I could see and understand things that a "normal" person living an enviably normal life could not. It was as if a window of perception had opened. I was driven to pay attention during this terrible time in order to see and learn things that I would never grasp again once the door was closed, and life went back to normal. Feeling this way gave me a sense of control when there was so much that was out of my control. I know this all sounds a little contradictory, but that it's the nature of life and death. The dark and the light exist side by side, all the time.

My sister and I were on the outs when the murder occurred. Six months before, she had subjected me to a brutal verbal attack. She accused me of hating my father. She asserted that I was so disgusted by him that I would do anything to avoid being around him. That last accusation was news to me, since I had just visited Dad a couple of weeks earlier. No matter what I said, or how I tried to defuse the situation, she escalated, until her eyes were slitted with contempt and hatred. I was utterly broadsided, though I shouldn't have been, as she had already subjected me to a lifetime of emotional and verbal abuse—often for no discernible reason.

Devastated, I drove home in the pouring rain. I don't know how I got home without killing myself in a car accident. On the advice of a friend, I called Dad and asked him if he had ever felt that I had treated him with disgust or hatred. He was confused, and asked where all of this was coming from. I didn't tell him, but I think he kind of figured it out for himself in the ensuing months. One day, as we were driving home from lunch, I eagerly told him about my involvement in a mentoring program for at-risk teenagers. He was pleased. After a long pause, he asked if I'd spoken with my sister, and I replied that I hadn't, for some time. He paused again, then he said something that astonishes me to this day. His words were as follows: "I don't think your sister gets it. YOU get it."

He didn't elaborate. He didn't have to; I understood what he meant.

When my sister showed up at my aunt's the day after the murder, I could tell she still harbored a simmering resentment against me. I set that aside and hugged her because our father had just been murdered. She barely hugged me back. In the ensuing years, we did have some good times together, but after that horrific attack I avoided any sort of true intimacy with her. Maybe not the bravest choice, but it was a protective choice, and I did it because above all I wanted to maintain a relationship with my two nieces—her daughters.

A tremendous betrayal came some years afterward. I cannot discuss it here due to legal considerations. It broke my heart. I realized finally that I had avoided addressing my mounting apprehension because my fear of loss of love was so profound. After a year of grief, terror, and shock, I resolved to rectify the situation. It took years, but today I am free of my sister's destructive influence, and I am the better for it. I only say this to warn survivors that violent death can make one vulnerable to various types of exploitation or abuse by family members. Be very careful.

Also I had a friend of many years who was a recovering addict. She had really turned her life around, but personal problems lingered. She was obese, having switched from one addiction to another. It was really annoying to be lectured about why I shouldn't really be eating or enjoying one sort of food or another. When she was on yet another one of her absurd diets, I suffered. She had terrible breath from the Atkins Diet. It was really hard to sit next to her, or across the table from her. When she was starving on an 800-calorie-a-day liquid diet, her eyes would follow to my mouth every morsel of food I was eating. She would tell me she wasn't really hungry at all, yet I could hear her belly moaning and grumbling from across the table. I ate so fast I got really painful stomach aches.

She also had a lot of unconscious nervous tics from the damage the drugs had done. I was already jumpy, and watching her twiddle her thumbs or click her tongue at the speed of light made me even more nervous.

But the worst thing was her son. She had him with her during his first two years of life, while she was still an addict. She left him with her ex while she got clean. Nine years later, she wanted him back, so that she could start some sort of ideal life with him. She sued for custody, and after a messy legal battle, won him back. She moved close to my neighborhood after a psychic in Sedona gave her some vague instruction to do so.

Her kid was seriously messed up his entire life. As he got older, things got scarier. I felt physically threatened several times. He swore at me. Visits to my friend's house became something I dreaded.

The U.S. Military's suicide rate surpassed combat deaths in 2012.

Bill Chappell
NPR, 1-14-2013

It never really leaves you, but you learn to enjoy life because that is what you have; it is a gift they could not see.

Myra

The many tapestries of order that permeate one's daily life become apparent only when one loses them, or oneself in them.

Robert A. Neimeyer

After a while, he turned violent. Destroyed things in my friend's house. Physically attacked her a time or two. This young man was built like a refrigerator, so none of this was easily ignored.

I was torn by my loyalty to my friend, even though my therapist and my friends told me to get away. This friend was so supportive after the murder and failed trial. I felt it would be wrong to turn my back on her. In retrospect, I think I knew as early as two months after the murder that the friendship was on life-support. That it was an unhealthy bond. Then, four years after the murder, her son got into some serious legal trouble.

At first my friend was saying all the right things. Her response to the event seemed healthy and self-protective.

Three weeks later, everything had changed. She blame-shifted. Put him on a pedestal. Minimized the seriousness of the crimes he had committed. At the time, I was feeling really good. I had just gotten back from a wonderful trip.

The future looked promising. I was exultant. When I saw that she was reverting to the same old thought patterns, I regressed. I became very emotionally unstable. Up until that point, I hadn't realized how very fragile trauma had rendered me. It was TERRIFYING. It was as if in one fell swoop, I returned to the time of the murder. I felt like I had done all of the hard work in therapy for nothing. That night I cut her off. I had my first incidence of PTSD. I called three friends who endorsed my decision. They later told me that I sounded just as I had immediately after the murder—breathless, panicked, confused, scared.

There I was, four years later, rebuilding my life, experiencing some distance from that horrific event, and enjoying extended periods of normalcy. Suddenly I felt I was back at Square One. It was a perilous time, indeed. Messed me up for another year, at least. Suffice it to say that I remain ruthless. In the intervening years, this friend has tried to renew contact. I did not respond. Finally she caught me on the phone, and I told her the truth. She was shocked and hurt, but didn't want to discuss anything in detail. Her

I make a schedule mentally to fill my days and nights and stay in contact with my friends.

Myra

reaction validated my decision. I'm the sort of person who will try and try to make things work, but when I decide that enough is enough, I'm gone in sixty seconds. Forever.

Myra

I am planning for my future, both financially and emotionally. I make a schedule mentally to fill my days and nights and stay in contact with my friends. I am getting lots of exercise and looking back trying to concentrate in my happier moments with my husband. It is not always easy, and when I backslide I see it right away and try to fix it. It never really leaves you, but you learn to enjoy life because that is what you have; it is a gift they could not see.

Austin

Nothing has really changed for me. Brad's death has given me another way to practice my belief (all is part of the drama of life). I think in some ways my belief has given strength to others. But it is also possible that others may see me as cold and uncaring. As a whole my confidence in my spiritual beliefs has given out positive vibrations. I was not lost in my own grief and was able to support others.

Louise

Revisiting my husband's death 50 years later has brought up some tears, some lack of ability to concentrate. Talking to my sister, brother, daughter and a friend or two has allowed me to talk about things that I've never been able to before. I found myself seriously considering whether or not to get copies of the court record during which the accident was discussed. I haven't decided whether it would be good to do or not.

It seems I have idealized him some, as I can't think of many negative things in our marriage or life. Or the things I may have disliked then, looking back, don't seem like problems.

Revisiting my husband's death 50 years later has brought up some tears, some lack of ability to concentrate.

Louise

What I have done to counter this "don't talk about it event" is to be a vehicle for me and others to tell their stories and what helps them live with what has happened.

Connie

Connie

What I have done to counter this "don't talk about it event" is to be a vehicle for me and others to tell their stories and what helps them to live with what has happened. I know of few other events that render people so utterly powerless than losing someone in a violent way. At the hands of another or at their own self-homicide. In helping others, I believe we do help ourselves. We also become powerful again in such powerlessness. Doing nothing just isn't an option that I promote for myself or others. What people decide to do is quite personal and must have meaning for them as well. I do not want folks to be alone like my family was. I don't want families to break apart the way mine did. I am pleased to know that I, through my commitment to make a difference in my sister's name, have done so.

You may want to read the article included at the end of this section from Deborah Spungen's book, *And I Don't Want to Live This Life: A Mother's Story of Her Daughter's Murder.*

Preparation for Step Five

We will ask you to spend some time getting ready for the next step. In doing so, we ask that you gather information and items that tell us more about your loved ones. Step Five will introduce your loved ones to us, to tell us about who they were and what was important to them. What was your relationship with them? Add as much as you would like here. What we have found helpful for you is NOT to include how they died. Use this section to represent who they were and what they meant to you while they were alive.

Now is the time to listen to the audio CD, Step Four, or you may read the text that follows. You may download an audio version at http://svlp.org/resources.html.

Step Four Closing Exercise

To get ready for this experience, sit in a comfortable chair in a quiet place where you will not be interrupted . . . then place your feet flat on the floor. . . . Sit forward and lean back with your shoulders resting on the back of your chair.

Place your hands on the upper part of your chest . . . gently, one on top of the other . . . and begin first by just noticing . . . the weight of your hands resting on your chest. . . . Make sure that your arms are not resting on the arms of the chair to get the full feel of the weight of your hands on your chest. . . . Now . . . notice the slight movement of your hands from your own breathing. . . . Again, you may find that closing your eyes helps you to focus more on these slight sensations.

*Now . . . take a deep breath in through your nose and **hold it** . . . . for as long as you can . . . and when you are ready . . . form your mouth into an O . . . and slowly breath out . . . let that air go . . . all the way out. . . . Then relax . . . and . . . slump . . . keeping your hands in place . . . just slump . . . like a rag doll . . . letting those muscles go . . . and relax . . . notice how well that chair is supporting you . . . with nothing you need to do . . . no place to go . . . you can just to let go . . . and relax.*

Passive Progressive Relaxation

Allow any thoughts or worries to enter your mind, but direct them out with each breath. Imagine troubling thoughts as a current of water that can be channeled out of you as you slowly exhale. After a few moments, begin focusing your attention on your toes. Think about how they feel. Think about the walking you have done today, and about how your feet and toes can now rest. Imagine the tension and pressure of walking or running as being drained out, flowing out of your feet.

Try visualizing the flow of tension running down your calves. Feel the flow draining out of you like water out of a drain spout or like syrup out of a bottle. Find images that you can visualize clearly that convey this notion. Move up your legs and continue your slow, deep breathing. Imagine your legs as large rags that are wet and limp. Feel your legs get heavy and relaxed. Continue this relaxation process moving up through your buttocks, stomach, back, and chest. Feel the heaviness in your stomach as the muscles let go of the tension. Let the sinking feeling spread throughout your abdomen. Allow any tension to gather and flow down your arms. Let it drain from your head and face and, like melting wax, flow down to your arms and hands and out of your fingers. Roll your head from side to side and feel the tensions breaking loose and flowing down and out.

Take a deep breath and as you exhale, feel your arms and hands heavy with the flow of residual tension. See the tension draining out like warm butter. Imagine squeezing out the last bit of tension and stress from your shoulders down to each finger.

Take a deep, satisfying breath and go back over your entire body and search for any remaining tension. Examine your forehead, jaw, and neck. Carefully imagine the stress and tension leaving the muscles of your back and any place that you think might be trapping some residual tension. Focus on it and allow it to feel warm and heavy. Try visualizing or imagine feeling all the tension dissolving or evaporating like alcohol in an open dish. Feel the warmth dissolving the tension like warm water dissolves salt. Let it be washed away.

To improve and practice the power of breathing, practice by taking deep

breaths in and holding them for as long as you can, in and out of your day.

One at a time, with normal breaths in between deep breaths.

And whenever you are ready, take your time, open your eyes, and slowly look around, noticing where you are. Take your time getting up and moving on with your day.

Read the following Excerpt and see Additional Reading in Appendix III

And I Don't Want to Live This Life:

A Mother's Story of her Daughter's Murder

by Deborah Spungen

I often wonder what people are thinking when they say, "You'll get over it." Sometimes it sounds to me as if they are talking about a case of mumps or my despair at income tax time. But what can they mean when they say it about my grief? Maybe they mean that grief is just an interruption in life. Their theory seems to be that life is basically happy—buying stuff, working, watching TV—but that a time of death and grief is an unnatural, sad time in that happy life.

I cannot agree with that view.

Time can lessen the hurt; the empty place we have can seem smaller as other things and experiences fill our life; we can forget for periods and feel as if our loved one didn't die; we can find sense in the death and understand that perhaps this death does fit into a bigger design in the world; we can learn to remember the good and hold on to that.

But we cannot "get over it," because to get over it would mean we were not changed by the experience. It would mean we did not grow by the experience. It would mean that our loved one's death made no difference in our life.

There is an interesting discussion in the Talmud and ancient Jewish writing. Those Jews had the custom of rending their garments—literally tearing their clothes—to symbolize the ripping apart that death brings. But the question was raised—after the period of mourning—could you sew the garment up and use it again? The teachers answered yes, but when you mended it, you should not tuck the edges under so it would look as if it had never been torn. This symbolized the fact that life after grief is not the same as before. The rent will show. The next question was, can you sell that garment? The teachers answered no. The rending and mending of our life is ours and others cannot wear it.

No, we don't get over it. We change and grow. Our life has a difference which is ours alone. Perhaps we can help each other make that difference, the kind of difference that increases the world's supply of compassion, love, and healing.

Adapted from *Reflections About Time and Change* by Dennis Klass
(copyright 1983; used with permission)

This page intentionally left blank. You are encouraged to use it for writing your story or keeping notes.

STEP FIVE

Your Loved One

This is one of my favorite steps for you. It is a favorite, as I get to hear and meet your loved ones. In this step of your Journey, we ask that you tell us about their life and your relationship with them.

Survivors tell us that few people ask about who their loved ones were and what was important to them. They instead ask for updates on the death of the loved one or the ongoing legal case.

For some of you we fully acknowledge and respect that finding positive memories and experiences of your loved ones may be much more difficult as their lives and yours were much more troubled. It may be that you will need to go to baby memories.

One mother who had a troubled story of her teenage son brought in a picture of the two of them adoring each other when he was an infant.

We also know that for many survivors, the horrific nature of the loss is both overwhelming and absorbing.

What has happened to our loved ones gets to be in the front of our minds. Who they were and what they represented gets overshadowed by how they died.

So we ask that you focus here on who they were, what they valued and your relationship to them. We believe by helping to pull this information to the front of your attention, you will be able to experience those memories more.

There is so much we do not have control over, but this is one area that no one can take from you. Your telling us who they were acts as a natural counterbalance to the thoughts and images of how they died.

Many of you also have expressed that you worry that your loved ones will be forgotten. We want to know them. We want to help remember them, too.

The story of the life of the victim gains ascendancy and becomes stronger than the story of their dying.
Edward Rynearson, MD

In Hamlet, Shakespeare wrote: *There's rosemary, that's for remembrance.*

89

This is where we ask you to tell us about them. This remembering will aid us in planning how we want to keep them living in our world in some way. But more on that plan later.

Now, it is enough to just tell us who they were. Take as much time as you need to tell us more about your loved ones.

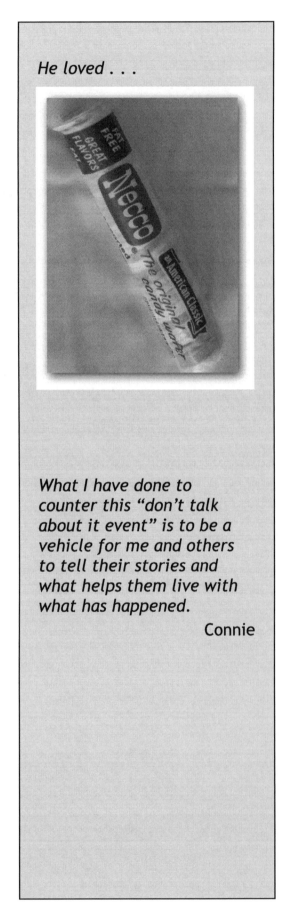

He loved . . .

What I have done to counter this "don't talk about it event" is to be a vehicle for me and others to tell their stories and what helps them live with what has happened.

Connie

STEP FIVE, QUESTION ONE

Who was your loved one?

I remember saying once that I was kidnapped by the death of not only my sister, but by all of the stories I was so intimately involved with in my work.

I was so consumed that I lost sight of health and relationships needs.

Fun was indeed out of the question. I made sure that I didn't laugh; what I was doing was the most important and I believe most needed activity of my entire life.

Connie Saindon

I don't want my life to be defined by Dad's murder; I want to be refined by it.

Marina

Survivor Voices

STEP FIVE, QUESTION ONE

Dee

Tara was my sister's oldest. I was twelve when she was born; my sister was almost sixteen. Tara was "my girl." We had the most incredible relationship. Tara was 14 months old when her young father was killed in a car crash. My sister was seventeen years old, widowed with two children: Tara, 14 months old, and Valerie, one month old. Life was not easy for my sister, which made things hard for her kids, which eventually totaled four.

Tara was an incredible big sister and at times played parent to her siblings. She took on many responsibilities at a young age, and that made her aware of so much. She loved her family. She was so special to my children, who were so young. She loved school. She loved to fish. She loved music and wrote songs and lyrics. She loved to paint and loved photography. She collected crosses. She served as Acolyte in her church. Her faith in God was very strong. She was very thoughtful and kept journals of her inner thoughts and feelings about life. We have these journals still.

When she died, she was studying in college to go into the medical profession. She loved helping people. She worked as a medical assistant at the local hospital. She was charitable to many. She had a gentle, determined, boundless spirit. I miss her terribly.

Elena

My brother was exactly 2 years younger than me. Our little sister didn't come along until he was ten so growing up it was the two of us and we managed to get into quite a bit of mischief together. He loved to play outside and hated that we had to take naps. One summer day when he was about four, I decided he was right not to want to nap so we snuck out the bedroom

> *Tara was an incredible big sister and at times played parent to her siblings. She took on many responsibilities at a young age, and that made her aware of so much. She loved her family.*
>
> *When she died, she was studying in college to go into the medical profession. She loved helping people.*
>
> Dee

window. Unfortunately, he broke his leg while we were out and was stuck in a cast the rest of the summer and into fall. That was even more torture for him because he couldn't run and play. I had a great deal of guilt over this because I had orchestrated our adventure and spent much of that summer hanging out with him.

Summertime was our favorite time of year. We learned to swim together, spending mornings with our friends at the pool and afternoons in the back yard playing on our swing set under a huge avocado tree. We had an old WWII parachute that we draped over the swing set so it became a huge tent for us. My brother was always dressed up as some king or character; in summer time he was GI Joe. Dad found an old WWII army radio with head phones and my brother spent his time sitting on a swing glider pretending he was on an airplane.

He also loved to take things apart and put them back together again. One day he spent a whole afternoon lying under the dining room table . . . all I could see were his lower legs and high-top sneakers sticking out. The table was never the same again once he was done with it.

I remember how he hated rainy days. I remember him one day wearing his cowboy hat, a little red vest and a holster with a silver gun. When it rained he'd sit at the window and sadly look outside, hoping it would stop.

No one knew about different learning disabilities in those days, and it wasn't until I was an adult that I came to realize that his challenges with school were because he had dyslexia.

I, on the other hand, did very well and was a bit of an overachiever. Phillip had to constantly hear "Why can't you be like your sister?" or "W hy don't you study harder?" from my parents and from the teachers who had taught me before him. Even I knew that was hurtful; I couldn't understand why they were insisting my brother be me.

As we got older, a good part of his summer was spent going to tutoring. I missed the freedom

My brother was exactly 2 years younger than me.

He loved to take things apart and put them back together again.

I remember how he hated rainy days.

My brother loved to joke around and he had a great sense of humor, often at my expense.

He worked for a nuclear energy company who had chosen him to go to Sweden and learn about a new reactor they were going to utilize.

My last words to him were, "I love you, please call me when you return."

Elena

summer used to mean for us, and I noticed he began to hate school. Sometimes we'd just walk home together and he'd not want to talk.

We moved in 1967, and for 1 year he and I were attending different schools because there were no openings for him at the Catholic school I attended. The next year we were together again; I was 12 and he was 10.

There was a girl from the old school he had attended who would be going home from her school in the opposite direction in which we were going. For some reason she did not like him and she'd be very mean to him when we passed each other. He never talked back to her or did anything to defend himself from her. One day she actually spit at him. I wanted to kill her at that moment and had tunnel vision. My brother cried, but I grabbed her by her clothes and told her to take me to her home.

Her house was not far. Her mother must have seen us coming up because she was already at the door when we arrived. I pushed her to her mother so hard the girl went flying past her and landed on the floor. I yelled at her mother and told her to keep her stupid daughter away from my brother. The girl never bothered us again, but that day my brother and I cried all the way home. Neither one of us wanted to tell Mom what happened. I wonder now how many other things happened to him that went unsaid.

My brother loved to joke around and he had a great sense of humor, often at my expense. One morning while I was still dressed in my pajamas the mail had arrived. I thought I could just run out to the box quickly and check without being seen by the neighbors (I was shy) so I did, but my brother locked the door behind me. I went running as fast as I could to the back door, but he locked that, too. Finally the only way I could get in was to climb through a window he opened in the front of the house. He was rolling on the floor, in tears from laughing. I had to sit next to him and laughed too, once I made it inside.

Once high school began for me, we spent much less time together, and we went in different directions. Just after high school my brother joined the navy. These were actually good years for him in that he really loved aviation mechanics and the travel he experienced. He was on an aircraft carrier, and his tour took him to Australia and Hong Kong. He was very handsome and looked really sharp in his navy pea coat.

My brother was never at a shortage for girlfriends, but the ones he liked most were ones I could not tolerate. They were selfish and narcissistic. I told him as much, but he said I just didn't want him to be happy. That hurt and I stopped saying anything.

He married one of them very young, and they had a son together. After he was discharged from the navy, he worked as a mechanic on aircraft. I don't know where he got the idea to go back to school, but he did, in addition to working and raising his son. It was not long before his wife left him for some other man.

I was so proud of my brother. He really struggled with the classes he was taking, with custody fights with his wife and working, but he managed to graduate as an electrical engineer.

There was a brief period of time when he moved back home after his divorce. My brother was constantly snooping through my sister's belongings, and he had found a 3-foot-long plastic tube on my sister's desk. He thought it a great idea to use it as a straw for his beer.

He was walking around the house shirtless and tanned with torn-up jeans and wearing an old crocodile Dundee-style hat. I'll never forget the look on his face when I told him it was used in her fish tank for a filter. He quickly recovered with an "oh, well" and continued enjoying his beer.

My brother married again, and this one was even worse than the first, having another son with her at her insistence. Still he made many good memories with his sons as they were a constant priority for him. He enjoyed cooking, scuba diving, hang gliding, cycling, and surfing—anything in the sun. He was a true California kid.

He moved to Seattle, Washington, because his wife, a pilot, had a work opportunity there. They divorced a couple of years later. My brother had been very involved in his son's life as she travelled all the time.

When they divorced, she moved back to Los Angeles and took their son with her. My brother remained in Washington because his job there paid well and because at the time there were no engineering jobs in Southern California. The last memories I have of him before he died were those of increasing bitterness with life. He called less and less, and when he did he was argumentative and hostile.

The last time we spoke he was more upbeat. He worked for a nuclear energy company who had chosen him to go to Sweden and learn about a new reactor they were going to utilize. They wanted him to be responsible for the entire project. I told him I was so proud of him, and that I was jealous that I couldn't go, too. I felt as if I was talking to my brother from many years before and that the darkness he was in was fading away. My last words to him were, "I love you, please call me when you return."

In Memoriam

You rose above impoverished childhood and used your innate intelligence and drive to become one of the first Hispanics to gradate as a 2nd lieutenant from officer candidate school. After years of toiling for others in the aerospace industry, you realized that you were smarter than many of your superiors and founded your very own high-tech electronics company.

Even after you became an enormously successful man—one who walked with presidents and advised corporate titans—you never forgot your humble beginnings. You reached out and tirelessly mentored young Hispanics who dared to dream as you once dreamed, and provided for your loved ones beyond your wildest imaginings.

You "phenomenated" us, and in return we promise to never forget you.

Your Loved Ones

Marina
On this one, I'd love to use the tribute I put in his local paper after we lost the trial:

In Memoriam

Over eight years have passed since your tragic death. We think of you often, and we know that there are many in this beautiful desert valley who miss you as deeply as we do. We will never forget that you lived a life like no other.

You rose above impoverished childhood and used your innate intelligence and drive to become one of the first Hispanics to graduate as a 2nd lieutenant from officer candidate school. After years of toiling for others in the aerospace industry, you realized that you were smarter than many of your superiors, and founded your very own high-tech electronics company.

Even after you became an enormously successful man—one who walked with presidents and advised corporate titans—you never forgot your humble beginnings. You reached out and tire-lessly mentored young Hispanics who dared to dream as you once dreamed, and provided for your loved ones beyond your wildest imaginings.

Though you were betrayed in death by numb minds, and mocked long after by false piety and maudlin sentiment, your powerful legacy lives on in the hearts of those who love and remember you. We will carry the truth with us as long as we are fortunate to breathe air. We honor you every day by living all who wronged you into irrelevance.

A surprising event which occurred three weeks before your birthday on April 17th reassured us that the wheel which turns Life's own brand of justice continues to revolve, whether we are aware of it or not. May the wheel continue its implacable circuit and prove that man cannot escape his innate nature, and is often his own worst enemy in the end.

With this in mind we look towards the future with renewed hope and trust that with time and tide,

My husband was a man's man, He loved camping, fishing, boating, and hiking. He loved all things military and loved his time in the service.

He loved nature and was a bit of a loner. He loved to read and watch old movies. He recorded over 700 movies and had a card catalog of his movies by title, director, and if they won Academy Awards.

Myra

our shared dream will come to pass. You "phenomenated" us, and in return we promise to never forget you.

Your Loved Ones

Myra

My husband was a man's man. He loved camping, fishing, boating, and hiking. He loved all things military and loved his time in the service. His greatest time of his life was when he was in Vietnam. He said he should have died there. He went in early, at 17, and was offered Officer's Candidate School. He was very intelligent. But he went AWOL for a girl and lost his top-secret clearance in the NSA, and this was his greatest disappointment.

He loved tinkering with things and could fix just about anything. He was creative and funny. He loved to cook and shop for his meals. He loved being the caretaker. He made my lunch every day and put a note in it. He never made much money; he undervalued himself and his talents.

He loved nature and was a bit of a loner. He loved to read and watch old movies. He recorded over 700 movies and had a card catalog of his movies by title, director, and if they won Academy Awards. He loved '40s music and wished he had been born earlier so he could have fought in WWII. He loved watching battle movies from WWI and WWII. He never wanted to watch movies about Vietnam.

He hated doctors and dentists. He had bad teeth; he was very handsome, but with his bad teeth he felt he was not attractive. He was wrong!! He drank too much at the end; it changed him. He was my best friend, and I attribute most of what I know to him. He was so smart and such a good man. I miss him.

He was a dedicated person who stood up for the underdog. I liked him because he was a rebel like me and didn't fit into the family "norm."

Austin

He was a lot of fun; he enjoyed other people, social activities. We always had a really good time when we got to dance.

Louise

She truly was a sweet, kind person who was well-known for doing little kind deeds to make people smile or cheer them up.

She was born a preemie, which was a big deal in 1944. The saying was "she was so tiny that she could fit in a tea cup."

Connie

Austin

Much of my nephew's life has been published in the newspapers. And is on his Web site. He was an independent photojournalist covering a teacher's uprising in Oaxaca, Mexico. He traveled a lot and I didn't see him much. I had gotten closer to him in the last couple of years. He told me about some of his adventures, but most of his interests and activities I learned from his mother, Kathy. He was a dedicated person who stood up for the underdog. I liked him because he was a rebel like me and didn't fit into the family "norm."

Louise

He was a lot of fun—he enjoyed other people, social activities. We always had a really good time when we got to dance. I think he enjoyed being married and having a family. I loved to cook for him because he really enjoyed good food. He was particular about his clothes and appearance and always liked to be neat and clean. He bought me nice clothes for gifts and surprises. I could scarcely believe when we got married that he expected me to iron his socks and underwear like his mother had—she had a mangle (ironing machine) so it was pretty easy. I did it, but I was happy not to, later on. I wasn't as particular about housekeeping as his mother, but he didn't complain. I hate to dust, and one day I went in the bedroom and there in the dust on his dresser he had written my name with his finger. We had a laugh over it.

Connie

She truly was a sweet, kind person who was well-known for doing little kind deeds to make people smile or cheer them up. For example: She would pick May flowers that grew wild, make a bouquet, and give them to a neighbor. None of us can remember her being disagreeable or arguing. She did not do what most of us did and that was fight with each other. Counting Mom and Dad, there were ten of us. I was the second oldest and she was the third oldest. She struggled in school, so attending Beauty College was a perfect match for her. She loved fixing peoples' hair and had worked on several people for my wedding.

She was born a preemie, which was a big deal in 1944. My parents didn't have a car and lived quite a way from the hospital. It was quite an ordeal to get to the hospital when she was born, and then again for the return visits needed due to her size. The saying was "she was so tiny that she could fit in a tea cup." Henceforth, she got her nickname "Tiny."

STEP FIVE, QUESTION TWO

What was it like to present your loved one? How was that different from your previous focus on them? How was it to listen to others tell about your loved one? If you read the survivor stories in this book, how was it to read about who their loved ones were?

Survivor Voices

STEP FIVE, QUESTION TWO

Dee
It was very uplifting remembering Tara's life and to share it with others. It was nice to think again of who she was and how she lived her life and loved her family. But the sadness of losing the future with her was felt.

I loved hearing others share about their loved ones and the joy in the words written about them. We are taken back to the time before we lost them. For a few moments things were restored in the telling—important things, not to be forgotten.

Elena
I had not thought of my brother's life since he died, only how he was during the last year before he took his life: bitter and angry. Telling his story was like opening an old trunk full of treasures I had put away long ago. My brother was much more than the day he died, and I had not allowed myself to enjoy that person. It was the first time in 19 years I could remember my brother and laugh at the good times we shared. I got my brother back and it was liberating, like getting out of a thick fog.

Also in sharing I began to realize that his life was a difficult one and that he had suffered much. It helped me to stop thinking only about what happened to all of us because of his death, but to try to understand the utter loneliness he must have been feeling at the end. I began to grieve him differently, not with frustration and confusion but with compassion.

The stories shared by others were amazing, and I found we were all having the same experience: remembering how a person lived was healing and in a sense gave that person back to us.

It was very uplifting remembering Tara's life and to share it with others.

Dee

I had not thought of my brother's life since he died, only how he was during the last year before he took his life: bitter and angry. Telling his story was like opening an old trunk full of treasures I had put away long ago.

The stories shared by others were amazing, and I found we were all having the same experience: remembering how a person lived was healing and in a sense gave that person back to us.

Elena

It felt really good to present Dad to the group. I didn't have time to feel sad, because I was so busy trying to fit in everything I had to say about him. I felt proud and happy when I finished.

Marina

Marina

It felt really good to present Dad to the group. I didn't have time to feel sad, because I was so busy trying to fit in everything I had to say about him. I felt proud and happy when I finished. I was warm with pride and admiration for him. For a brief time, I felt that I wasn't so alone. The approbation from members of the group was pleasing.

I realized that my dad had lived quite the life. He lived the life of three men, not one. He crammed a lot of fun and accomplishment into his sixty-eight years. For years before Dad's death, I had spent so much time worrying about him. After he had a stroke at the end of 1992, he suffered from clinical depression. His doctors had told him that the stroke was most likely caused by his heavy consumption of alcohol. He had every chance to make a wondrous recovery. Instead, he chose to continue drinking, which further weakened his capacities, and worsened his depression. This opened the door to the predator who murdered him five years into their relationship. He had many opportunities to cut his bond with her. Two opportunities to make police reports after incidents of physical abuse and property destruction. Out of pride, shame, and a self-destructive need to maintain control, he did not. We knew nothing about the physical abuse during the length of their relationship. I suffered a lot of guilt and self-recrimination about that after Dad was taken from us. Now I understand that these feelings were not in any way justified. How could I have known? As with murder, the abuse didn't fit into any existing frame of reference.

The presentation helped me to see my dad as a totally self-determining individual. It got the good stuff out of the way, so that I could begin to see him in a less-idealized light. He made his own choices. This is crucial, because after we lost the trial, I was in agony. I remember being in the car with my boyfriend, driving away from the courthouse.

I was in total shock. I felt I would die, right then and there. Overwhelmed, I expressed an inarticulate rage directed at both my dad and his murderer. Talk about being torn in half emotionally!

I cry when I think of what an amazing man he was.

Myra

It made me feel warm and like smiling when I looked over all the photos.

Louise

Frustrated, my boyfriend said, "Your father may not have chosen his death, but he chose the path that led to it."

The truth of it hit me like a sledge hammer. No, my dad did not deserve to be murdered like a steer in a slaughterhouse.

But he was not an unwitting innocent, either. He craved chaos and conflict in his relationships. He was a great guy in many ways, and had a lot of good folks around him, including former girlfriends who kept in touch with him right up until the end of his life. But those women had curtailed their romantic relationships with him. In the end, Dad found himself with an abusive druggie-grifter-con who happened to present passably well. He could have come to any of us for help once the abuse started. When we tried to intervene after she tore his house apart in a fit of rage, he shut us out.

The only reason I go into all of this is that with my dad, at least, it was important for me to see the "big picture." To see his life in all of its richness, its triumphs, and its dismal failures. I needed to feel the anger and the resentment as much as I needed to experience the pride, joy, and love.

Idealization is normal, and I did idealize him at first. But it didn't take me as far as I needed to go in order to release him so that I could live a full life once more.

Myra
I did this with Hospice; we made a book of things and presented our story to the group. It was a difficult experience, but healing at the same time. Even now, I cry when I think of what an amazing man he was.

Austin
It was good. Presenting gave me a warm feeling. Previous focus was on the pain of Brad's death. I did not read about other people and who their loved ones were.

Louise
It made me feel warm and like smiling when I looked over all the photos, trying to pick out which ones to put here. Being married to my husband was a happy time. I'm glad I have good memories to look back on. I could talk about him if I had an interested audience.

Connie
I love talking about my sister and what she meant in this world. This has been just one more opportunity to do so. I love hearing the stories of other people, too.

Now it is time to listen to the audio CD, Step Five, or you may read the text that follows. You may download an audio version at http://svlp.org/resources.html.

Step Five Closing Exercise

To get ready for this experience, sit in a comfortable chair in a quiet place where you will not be interrupted . . . then place your feet flat on the floor. . . . Sit forward and lean back with your shoulders resting on the back of your chair.

Place your hands on the upper part of your chest . . . gently, one on top of the other . . . and begin first by just noticing . . . the weight of your hands resting on your chest. . . . Make sure that your arms are not resting on the arms of the chair to get the full feel of the weight of your hands on your chest. . . . Now . . . notice the slight movement of your hands from your own breathing. . . .

Again, you may find that closing your eyes helps you to focus more on these slight sensations.

Now . . . take a deep breath in through your nose and **hold it** *. . . . . for as long as you can . . . and when you are ready . . . form your mouth into an O . . . and slowly breath out . . . let that air go . . . all the way out. . . . Then relax . . . and . . . slump . . . keeping your hands in place . . . just slump . . . like a rag doll . . . letting those muscles go . . . and relax . . . notice how well that chair is supporting you . . . with nothing you need to do . . . no place to go . . . you can just to let go . . . and relax.*

Questions About 9/11

An old adage reads: "No Reason nor Rhyme."

But tell me God: "Was that his time?"

Why that meeting, that morning,

That room

Of all the buildings in Washington

To meet his doom

At the Pentagon

Consulting with three-star General Maud

Proposing a plan they now applaud?

Why couldn't he have finished

And begun walking away

To his car, far, far from

The horror of that

Cruel end?

When, when will I ever mend?

Muriel

The Cape of Grief

When you are ready, I would like you to imagine a garment that you are wearing . . . notice that this garment is a gown or a cape . . . and it is very heavy, black, and uncomfortable. This is the garment of your grief, or loss, that you bear. Pay attention to this heavy garment ... resting on your shoulders . . . and pressing against your body. . . . Feel how hot and uncomfortable this garment is to you. . . . Feel the rough texture and coarseness of the cloth against your skin. . . . Notice how deep this cloth penetrates. . . . Notice the deep discomfort for awhile . . . paying attention to your feelings of mad, sad, and scared.

Now. . . calling upon your own ability to use your healing, heart-breathing exercise . . . to come to help with this extra weight ... take a nice deep breath in and hold it . . . and then, out of your mouth . . . slowly release that breath . . . all the way out, to lighten the load of this burden, this cape. . . .

Notice how the weight on your body lifts . . . as it begins to lift from your shoulders and disappears over your head. . . . You may notice your cape becomes lighter and more delicate . . . and a shower of light . . . begins to pour down, all over your body. Not only does your cape feel lighter, but it may be warming you as well.

Feel the many tiny points of light penetrating your body . . . and note the increased protection and lightness of your new cape.

Enjoy this feeling . . . and this lightness . . . and remember that this experience is fully yours . . . so you know you can return to your lighter garment again, when you need to.

To improve the power of breathing, practice by taking deep breaths in

and holding them for as long as you can, in and out of your day.

One at a time, with normal breaths in between deep breaths.

Take your time to come back to the experience of being in the room . . . to your day . . . knowing you have strengthened your ability to feel lighter for a few moments of your day. . . .

This page intentionally left blank. You are encouraged to use it for writing your story or keeping notes.

What You Can't Forget

On the path of helping you learn to live with what has happened, we ask an important question. What is it that you keep seeing, or thinking, about how your loved one died? What comment, question, or event seems to repeat in your head more than others?

What you can't forget T-shirt.

As I mentioned earlier, what has happened is often beyond words, so drawing images may help. Get some quiet time, some time when you are alone and aren't interrupted, and remember to use your comforting breathing exercise when you want to take a break from this task.

Other survivors have told us that this can be one of the most difficult tasks to do. They also tell us it has been the most helpful task. The repetitive image or thought may lose its power when it is down on paper. The troubling repetition may decrease as well.

I also recommend that once you have completed all of the ten steps one time through, come back and repeat this step. And review the recollection of your loved one that you pulled together in Step Five. You may want to add some new things that come to mind.

The Challenge of Forgiveness

I'm not worrying about forgiveness; I am leaving that up to God.

> Sister of the murder victim; she and her husband were active in a religious group

We've extended forgiveness to the man who murdered Gerald and to the young girl who was the only witness. She came forward and said she lied. But we are having trouble forgiving the judge and the system.

> Conrad Moore

If my hand or arm had just been blown off, then people would understand. They'd see there's something wrong.

> David Griego

107

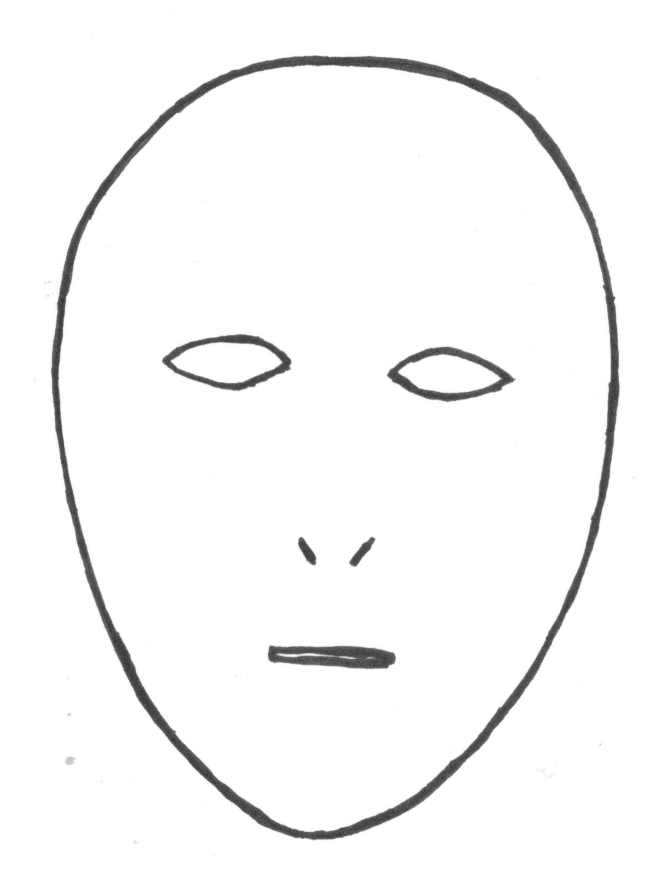

Step Six, Question One

What is it that you keep seeing, or thinking, about how your loved one died? What comment, question, or scene seems to repeat in your head more than others?

If words fail you, use a large piece of paper, or make a copy of the blank mask included on the adjacent page, to show what is inside you that you can't forget. Sit with a pencil, or markers or crayons, and put on paper what keeps repeating in your head.

Once you have completed this task, present this to someone who has been a support to you. Ask this person to see and hear what you have pulled together. If you are in therapy, ask your therapist to listen to your presentation as well. If you are in a support group, take turns to present this to others. As you begin to show what you have written or drawn, consider this question: How can your loved one help you present what you have prepared?

Survivor Voices

STEP SIX, QUESTION ONE

Dee

Tara was alone at a friend's house late at night studying for her college finals. She was viciously attacked by a man who forced his way into the house after Tara opened the door to look out after hearing someone yelling outside. She fought him in every room of the small house. The scene I keep seeing in my head is her lying naked on the bathroom floor, hands bound behind her back, helpless and dying. I want her to have never opened that door to see what was going on outside.

Elena

I had to go to my brother's house to settle his estate so I know what the room looked like, where the walls were cleaned and where the cushion of his office chair and the carpet were cut to remove the blood. I keep seeing that and I see that my brother was in that room far away from all of us who loved him. I realize he was feeling terribly alone and isolated. I remember that even while I was up there EVERY DAMN DAY it rained and how much that brought my brother down. He hated the rain. The worst image of all is that I see him in his aloneness putting the gun to his mouth and pulling the trigger, giving up.

Marina

My dad was bludgeoned with a lamp and possibly a phone; the blows disabled him. Then he was manually strangled to death. The DA said the inner tissue of the neck was heavily bruised, all the way around. This means that his killer kept adjusting her hands in order to get a better grip on her victim. The coroner noted that there was also a distinct possibility that the murderer stood on Dad's neck at some point in order to hasten his death.

Do you know that it takes two to four minutes to manually strangle a human being? That it is one of the most agonizing, personal ways to end someone's life? You really have to mean it in order to follow through with it. There are many, many opportunities to reconsider your actions as you listen to your victim fight for his or her life.

So I kept seeing her hands on his neck, digging in. His look of shock and terror as he looked into her black, opaque, pitiless eyes, and realized that this was it—that she meant to kill him. I heard him choking, gagging, and making horrible mewling noises. I flashed upon his hands up, protectively, when he first went down, trying to shield himself from the blows of the heavy brass lamp she used. She stuck him three times: once on top of the skull, once on each side. The coroner said that his tongue and lower lip were badly split, and that she probably kicked him hard in the mouth as he lay helpless on the floor.

The DA also said that there were fingernail marks on one side of Dad's neck. His girlfriend had two broken fingernails on the corresponding hand. I saw those blood-filled, crescent-shaped marks in my mind's eye for years afterward, without ever having seen a photograph. Unfortunately, I have a very good imagination.

The homicide detective told me that it looked as though the furniture in the master bedroom where Dad was killed had been moved around. There was a bottle of cleaning fluid on the mantel, a bottle I gave him after he had periodontal surgery, because it was especially effective at cleaning blood. That did a number on my head. I think the girlfriend figured out that a 10-ounce bottle wasn't going to do the job. She ended up using bath towels to clean up the blood as best she could. Wet towels with what looked to be faint bloodstains were later found in packing boxes in the hallway outside the master bedroom. (Dad was two weeks away from moving into a secure gated community, and the boxes had been packed and taped shut by the maid the morning before the murder.) Police also found wet, faintly bloody towels wrapped up in a bedroom area rug in the trunk of the girlfriend's car. The bundle was secured with a garden hose, of all things. Police also found her passport and the deed to her house in the car's glove compartment. Because of this, I believe the murder was premeditated.

Dad also had post-mortem drag marks and scrapes on his back. There were flattened areas on his body where blood had pooled. Like some insane window-dresser, she dragged him around as if he were a mannequin. It was unimaginable, yet it was way too easy to imagine. I also envisioned her hiding things, cleaning things, rushing about feverishly. The DA said there were numerous calls sometime after 11 p.m. from my dad's number to a cell number in Long Beach. It turns out that the cell phone belonged to a friend of hers. Not coincidentally, this same friend bailed her out of jail less than two days later.

"Manipulating the scene in order to support her story of accidental death" is how the homicide detective put it.

I have a mental picture of her screaming into the phone, then hanging up between calls in order to tweak her work a little further.

Myra

I was at the scene. I arrived just minutes after he shot himself. I went to get the neighbor and he called 911. My husband was gasping for air and blood was everywhere. I keep seeing his eyes in the chair where he shot himself. I also see his eyes at the trauma center where I said good-bye to him. I told him it was okay to go, a tear rolled down his check, and he was gone. These two scenes are what I see.

Austin

Unfortunately, the scene that I keep seeing is the Internet video of Brad's being shot, his wounded body with blood on it. The question that repeats in my mind is: "Why didn't he get out of that situation (people shooting at him and the protesters)."

Louise
I see his body (really just his face, neck, hands, and wrists) in the morgue, looking all waxy, stiff and unalive. I was relieved that there were no signs of being burned or injured skin, etc. Someone had taken his favorite suit, shirt, tie to the morgue to dress him in.

The thing that affected me a lot were all those people coming to my house, realizing later that they must have known more than I even suspected, and no one voiced the situation. Later it made me feel very naïve and stupid for not even thinking of the possibility that the accident might have involved him. It brings tears to my eyes just to type this.

I remember the scene at the cemetery and all the people that were there. Later I learned that some of my dearest friends had been there and not come up to me afterwards to let me know they had driven from another state, and I didn't even get a chance to experience their support. People just don't know what to say, at least at our young age, at that time. Still it did mean a lot to find out later that they had come.

Connie
What I kept seeing was her lying on the ground where she was left, alone. I know the place well enough; it is embedded in my mind. I see lots of trees, which is what Maine is noted for. I see a gravel road that people use to get into the dump. I also see his truck with the volunteer fireman emblem on the back of his truck.

STEP SIX, QUESTION TWO

Once you reveal what keeps repeating in your head, ask this next question: Where would I put myself in this situation, in this scene? If I could be there, where would I want to be?

The malevolent intent in deaths such as homicide and terrorism increases stressors.

Additional stressors can be:

- Reconciling how a loved one died
- Threat(s) may continue to exist
- Media making public what was private
- Crime-scene demands
- Victim identification
- Medical exam requirements
- Legal imperatives
- Security

PTSD is more severe and longer lasting when the trauma is of human design.
Buet & Smucker, 2006

Survivor Voices

STEP SIX, QUESTION TWO

Dee

If I could be there that night, I would want to be behind her telling her not to open the door. Just look out the window! At least, I would have wanted to have a weapon handy and help her fight back.

Elena

I would be right next to him, pushing the gun away. I would hold him and love him into the morning.

Marina

I had two conflicting versions of where I would put myself in the murder scene. Initially, I saw myself saving the day, attacking Dad's girlfriend and pulling her off of him. That felt good.

Later, a more realistic version of events replaced the idealized one. For one thing, my dad's girlfriend was pretty stocky. Also, I figured that she must have been completely adrenalized with rage, and the need to kill. He was a problem, and she meant to solve that problem once and for all. She would not hesitate to hurt or even kill anyone or anything that got in her way.

Realistically, I saw myself standing at the door to his bedroom, half-hidden by the doorjamb, staring at the scene in shock and disbelief, too terrified to intervene. Had she seen me, I would have run over an elephant in order to get away from her. Even if she hadn't seen me, I would have run for my life.

I visualized myself in a full-on sprint down the long hallway leading to the front door. Bursting outside and running into the pitch-black desert night down the long, dark street. Screaming for help, and never stopping.

If I could be there that night, I would want to be behind her telling her not to open the door.

Dee

I would be right next to him, pushing the gun away. I would hold him and love him into the morning.

Elena

I saw myself standing at the door to his bedroom, half-hidden by the doorjamb.

I visualized myself in a full-on sprint down the long hallway leading to the front door. Bursting outside and running into the pitch-black desert night down the long, dark street. Screaming for help and never stopping.

Marina

Myra

I really wish I had not seen him right after he shot himself. I wish I could just have seen him at the hospital. It was just so intense.

Austin

I guess I would be with him and tell him to get out of there. Tell him that his family would not want him to get hurt or killed.

Louise

I have a hard time imagining the scene where he actually might have been at the time of the explosion. I can't imagine myself being there. I knew nothing about what his work site looked like—the silo, the trailer/office, etc. So I can mostly picture what was in the newspapers and on TV. I believe everyone died instantly; if I had been there, he most likely would have been carried out of the silo dead, and I would not have been able to hold his hand, or give him a kiss, or say anything to him at the end.

If I had been on the site and had any intuition of it, I would have tried to get him to not go back to work after lunch, to be late, manufactured an excuse to keep him top-side for an extra ten minutes. Until this assignment I had never thought of this imaginary situation.

I have no doubt that my husband knew I loved him, and I knew he loved me.

Connie

I would form a cocoon around her on the ground with my body and just hold her so that she could feel my presence and my comforting her so she would not feel alone. I will never know the answer about why she was killed as he is now dead himself and if I asked him I wouldn't trust his answer. I have researched human behavior in hopes to come up with some understanding. I have collected some ideas that

> I wish I could just have seen him at the hospital.
>
> Myra

> If I had been there, he most likely would have been carried out of the silo dead, and I would not have been able to hold his hand, or give him a kiss, or say anything to him at the end.
>
> Louise

115

he had a mother that nagged him a lot and never felt good enough for, and he had some mental limitations. He was the guy that hung around the fire station. It has also been suggested that he might have killed another girl, and he had an uncle on the police force that may have gotten him off on other charges. And this last event, killing my sister, was an acceleration of developing crises he was having.

Now it is time to listen again to your audio CD using Step Six, or you may read the text that follows. You may download an audio version at http://svlp.org/resources.html.

Step Six Closing Exercise

To get ready for this experience, sit in a comfortable chair in a quiet place where you will not be interrupted . . . then place your feet flat on the floor. . . . Sit forward and lean back with your shoulders resting on the back of your chair.

Place your hands on the upper part of your chest . . . gently, one on top of the other . . . and begin first by just noticing . . . the weight of your hands resting on your chest. . . .

Now . . . notice the slight movement of your hands from your own breathing. . . .

Again, you may find that closing your eyes helps you to focus more on these slight sensations.

Now . . . take a deep breath in through your nose and **hold it** *. . . . . for as long as you can . . . and when you are ready . . . form your mouth into an O . . . and slowly breath out . . . let that air go . . . all the way out. . . . Then relax . . . and . . . slump . . . keeping your hands in place . . . just slump . . . like a rag doll . . . letting those muscles go . . . and relax . . . notice how well that chair is supporting you . . . with nothing you need to do . . . no place to go . . . you can just to let go . . . and relax.*

Continue taking deep breaths and holding them . . . in between normal breaths . . . and listen again as I read a poem . . . that I believe will be important to you.

This poem was written for you by Kyla Black.

I Never Got to Say Good-Bye

Bathrobe is still hanging on the door
Dirty socks still lying on the floor
Hairbrush sits beneath the mirror's frame
Strange to think the fingerprints remain

In an instant, life is not the same
The smile, the voice we never can reclaim
So unfair, so much more life to live
So hard to go on, much less forgive

I never got to say good-bye
Despite how many tears I cry
All I want to know is why
I never got to say good-bye

If there's a God in Heaven, please let them know
I never dreamed they'd have to go
Sometimes it's more that I can bear
To stay here when they're up there

Please tell them that I love them so
And it's so hard to let them go
I still wish as days go by
I'd had the chance to say good-bye

I never got to say good-bye
Despite how many tears I cry
All I want to know is why
I never got to say good-bye

Take your time to come back to the experience of being in the room . . . to your day . . . knowing you have strengthened your ability to feel lighter for a few moments of your day. . . .

Spiritual Beliefs

STEP SEVEN, QUESTION One

Let's review: Was it of value to you to remember who your loved one(s) was? Can you recall something about your loved one and not just how he or she died? If you read some of the other Survivor Voices, what words do you find that resonate with your experience?

It is extremely useful not only to hear oneself, but also to hear others who are experiencing similar trauma. . . . I learned that in working my way through tragedy, anything goes—as long as I do not do lasting harm to myself or others. I also got bits and pieces of knowledge from others with older cases regarding the legal process. This was invaluable.

Says Ana, who lost her brother 11/99

Veterans of Faith in most religions find something of an abiding presence in the midst of their longing and suffering. They experience their God or Higher Being not so much as a solution to their problem with grief, but as a companion who stands with them in the midst of it. This kind of faith gives strength.

Janice Lord
No Time for Goodbyes

Survivor Voices

STEP SEVEN, QUESTION ONE

Dee

I wonder what she was thinking. Was she thinking the disturbance could have been one of her siblings or her Mother? She was worried about some people who were threatening her Mother. It was very difficult to again visualize Tara in that situation. Its images are so awful. The "if onlies" so prevalent. To let these images out and process them full force, and especially to present them to others, has definitely been a release from deep within. These images and feelings kept inside forever can be so destructive in too many ways. I know that when you let bad things and feelings out into the light, they lose the power to dominate your thoughts and your life. It was stabilizing to know my thinking wasn't so different from others who have had these experiences. Their emotions echo my own. To know I'm not alone.

Elena

I have carried the image of how my brother died for years and never thought to tell anyone. It was too much to say those words to another and expect them to carry that with me. Sharing that memory was very painful yet such a huge release, like draining an abscess, it had to be done so I can heal from the inside out. The image that has been coming to me since sharing is that I am holding and loving my brother as if I can break through time and place as we know it and be there with him outside of what this world limits us to. A sense of transcendence of my love for him over space, time, and horror.

All the stories shared resonated with me. That awful common ground that we are powerless to change what happened, yet in sharing our story we somehow strip it of its power over us and we can interject our love into that moment. So healing.

Within two weeks of doing this exercise, the visions in my head just stopped. There was nothing more I could get out of them. It was as if they were trapped in my head, and putting them on paper gave them somewhere else to go.

Marina

I really try not to think about it, and really focus on our vacations and all of the good times. I know he would not want me to remember him like that.

Myra

It was like concretizing a small bit of the entire memory. The value to me is to let our daughter and son know more about the death of their father—but it is actually more letting them know how it affected their mother.

Louise

 **Marina**
Putting my vision of my father's murder on paper wasn't as hard as I thought it would be. It took less than an hour to fill that rather large white piece of paper right to its margins. I dumped everything from what I called the "mad merry-go-round" of death imagery. I paint porcelain, so I threw in some red splatters. I try not to turn away from anything. A visiting therapist who was sitting in on our group that night stared at the piece of paper and said, "How can you be standing there looking so normal with what you put on that paper?"

I replied, "That's nothing compared with what's in my head."

I felt strong and proud. Flooded with emotions, to be sure. It turned out to be quite a release. Within two weeks of doing this exercise, the visions in my head just stopped. There was nothing more I could get out of them. It was as if they were trapped in my head, and putting them on paper gave them somewhere else to go. To this day I can't quite believe that it happened. I thought I'd have to live with those images in my head forever.

 **Myra**
I really try not to think about it, and really focus on our vacations and all of the good times. I know he would not want me to remember him like that.

 **Austin**
It was a bit sad to complete the last step. Thoughts like it is too bad that Brad got killed and the images of his death. I haven't read other Survivors Voices yet.

 **Louise**
It was like concretizing a small bit of the entire memory. The value to me is to let our daughter and son know more about the death of their father—but it is actually more about letting them know how it affected their mother.

I have read the others survivor's stories. They seem to have a much more horrible experience. Some were personal attacks rather than an accident caused by someone I didn't even know. That seems to make a difference.

The fact that these were more fresh and current with the writers rather than 50 years ago lets me see how far I have come in putting distance between myself, the accident, the effects, etc. I don't feel as emotional as they seem in their accounts.

 **Connie**
It is easier every time I describe what I keep seeing. Every time I tell this story, new information and detail emerges. The image is increasingly outside of me. It has become less of a circulating image that I alone repeat and repeat. I also feel less alone and hope my truth will encourage others to tell their stories so they, too, won't be so alone with the worst thing that can happen to them.

When I remember the scene, I become more connected to all the ways her death has inspired and aided me in being a resource for so many others. I think she would be proud of what work has been done in her name. Thousands of people knew her. She may be "Tiny," but her work and heart is gargantuan.

STEP SEVEN, QUESTION TWO

Beliefs.

We know that change occurs for many folks and one area that can result in great challenge is one's spiritual/religious beliefs.

On the one hand some will be moved away from their "God" or spiritual support. Some may feel angry and not understand why the death of their loved one was God's will. Some will feel shame as they believe that Suicide is a Sin. Others may find increased comfort in their faith community.

What has happened for you? And remember, there are no right or wrong answers here.

Survivor Voices

STEP SEVEN, QUESTION TWO

 **Dee**
My faith really was not compromised. But I really wanted to know why! I did not blame the parents of the murderer. I held him alone responsible. I do believe this is Man's world and God gave man free will. This was this man's doing—not God's. Tara's faith and love of God was great. I know she is OK, now. We who are left, our suffering continues, not hers. She is free. What is hard is letting go of what would have been had she lived. I miss her. Her passing certainly set me on a quest to find my own spiritual path, which had less to do with religion than it does with finding my own life purpose and my own spirituality. It also made me determined to look inside myself and work to heal broken relationships with my family members, as best I could.

I worked to become able to take responsibility for my part only. But first I had to heal inside myself. First I had to learn how to focus on Tara's life and not her death. I learned that here. As far as my need to know why—I read a verse somewhere that said, "If we understand, things are as they are. If we do not understand, things are as they are." So I guess we come to accept things as they are in these cases.

 **Elena**
My "religion" was once just part of being who I was; if you're Mexican, you're Catholic. The day I was at my brother's house where he died, I found his suitcase thrown in a corner. In it I found a sweater I had given him the Christmas before. It smelled of his cologne. I broke down and did not know how I would go on; it was just too much. It was then that I sensed God's presence holding me. The best way to explain that experience is that I was crying and being heard and held and loved. That experience is what carried me and gave me the strength just

> *I do believe this is Man's world and God gave man free will. This was this man's doing—not God's.*
>
> Dee

> *My "religion" was once just part of being who I was; if you're Mexican, you're Catholic. The day I was at my brother's house where he died, I found his suitcase thrown in a corner. In it I found a sweater I had given him the Christmas before. It smelled of his cologne. I broke down and did not know how I would go on; it was just too much. It was then that I sensed God's presence holding me.*
>
> Elena

to be able to get up in the morning and move forward. That is when God became real to me and my religion became an expression of my faith in that God who carried me. It changed the trajectory of my life.

 **Marina**

Everything that happened strengthened and refined my beliefs. It became even clearer to me that there is no afterlife, and that there is no help for us from any supernatural power in this life. We are, each and every one of us, alone during our time in this world. It doesn't matter how many other folks surround us. We die alone.

There is no "greater meaning" in life, other than what we decide to believe for our own purposes.

What we call life's "meaning" is simply a reflection of our own subjective perceptions. "Meaning" is a mirror for our needs, our fears, our likes and dislikes.

Before the murder, I called myself an agnostic. I straddled the fence unhappily, because I did not wish to offend or displease others. I wanted too much for others to like me, but it was at the expense of my core beliefs, and my integrity. After we lost the trial, my heart and mind turned to ash. Everything I thought to be important or true was incinerated. I was unmoored. I didn't give a damn about anyone or anything. Nihilism ruled. I felt nothing but contempt for the values and beliefs our society holds dear.

Eventually, I decided to live as my true self. I felt I had nothing left to lose. It took a long time, but the pain and trauma forced a sort of metamorphosis. I feel a calm satisfaction in my beliefs now. I'm less defensive. When others try to force their own beliefs on me, I try to keep my own counsel, and just step aside. Each to his own.

Everything I thought to be important or true was incinerated. I was unmoored.

Eventually, I decided to live as my true self. I felt I had nothing left to lose.

Marina

My belief is very much a source of comfort. I believe that after death one goes on to the next chosen plane of existence.

Austin

My husband coming to me in the dream telling me that he will always love me has been sustaining to me.

Louise

Myra

I feel closer to God as I asked him to help me every day to get through this. I know I am stronger now and can see hope and joy in the future that I once could only see misery.

Austin

My belief is very much a source of comfort. I believe that after death one goes on to the next chosen plane of existence. I see death as a phase of life as a human—even violent death. I believe that before we are born we "chose" (as Spirit) what we will experience in the human form. I don't think that Spirit judges life experience. I think Spirit just wants to experience EVERYTHING. Therefore, no experience in what we call life is bad or wrong as to Spirit. But to us we need judgments in order for society to work.

Louise

I have never believed God "made" it happen; it wasn't a punishment, a "test" of faith. No one "sinned." It happened. In life, things happen. Sometimes there isn't a "Why," a reason. What matters is how we choose to deal with it—inside ourselves and in our outer behavior. My husband coming to me in the dream and telling me that he will always love me, the teachings of the Episcopal Church that God is Love, and the ongoing statements by my dad during my life that I am loved and guided have been sustaining to me.

My goal pretty much all my life has been to be a loving person. Then and now. At the time I felt a responsibility for raising my children with love and responsibility. At times I felt it was hard to be a single parent. But later, I found it was also hard at times to parent as a couple. The upside of being a single parent is that I could do things my way, without interference, compromise, or arguing. I couldn't be a father AND mother, but I could be the best Mother I could be. I think I did OK; my kids turned out to be good, kind, caring, intelligent people. They express appreciation and understanding regarding my being a single parent and the job I did.

Connie

I have more faith in human ability. I know so many folks that have learned to live with horrible things that have happened when they were vulnerable or when they were strong and humbled. I am honored to hear their stories and am deeply impressed with how they transformed themselves and others in their lives. They are truly heroes and I am humbled by their strength.

Now it is time to listen again to your audio CD using Step Six, or you may read the text that follows. *You may download an audio version at http://svlp.org/resources.html.*

Step Seven Closing Exercise

To get ready for this experience, sit in a comfortable chair in a quiet place where you will not be interrupted . . . then place your feet flat on the floor. . . . Sit forward and lean back with your shoulders resting on the back of your chair.

Place your hands on the upper part of your chest . . . gently, one on top of the other . . . and begin first by just noticing . . . the weight of your hands resting on your chest. . . . Now . . . notice the slight movement of your hands from your own breathing. . . .

Again, you may find that closing your eyes helps you to focus more on these slight sensations.

Now . . . take a deep breath in through your nose and **hold it** *. . . . . for as long as you can . . . and when you are ready . . . form your mouth into an O . . . and slowly breath out . . . let that air go . . . all the way out. . . . Then relax . . . and . . . slump . . . keeping your hands in place . . . just slump . . . like a rag doll . . . letting those muscles go . . . and relax . . . notice how well that chair is supporting you . . . with nothing you need to do . . . no place to go . . . you can just to let go . . . and relax . . . and continue to take deep breaths in between normal ones as I read this poem to you, author unknown.*

In Memory of You

I find an old photograph
And see your smile.
As I feel your presence anew,
I am filled with warmth
And my heart remembers love.

I read an old card
Sent many years ago
During a time of turmoil and
Confusion.
The soothing words written then
Still caress my spirit
And bring me peace.

I remember who you used to be
The laughter we shared
And wonder what you have become.
Where are you now,
Where did you go,
When the body is left behind
And the spirit is released to fly?

Perhaps you are the morning bird
Singing joyfully at sunrise,
Or the butterfly that dances

So carelessly on the breeze
Or the rainbow of colors
That brightens a stormy sky
Or the fingers of afternoon mist
Delicately reaching over the
Mountains
Or the final few rays of the setting sun
Lighting up the skies
Edging the clouds with a magical
Glow.

I miss your being
But I feel your presence,
In whatever form you choose to take,
However you now choose to be.

Your spirit has become for me
A guardian angel on high
Guiding, advising, and watching over
Me.

I remember you,
You are with me
And I am not afraid.

To improve the power of breathing, practice by taking deep breaths in

and holding them for as long as you can, in and out of your day.

One at a time, with normal breaths in between deep breaths.

Take your time to come back to the experience of being in the room . . . to your day . . .
knowing you have strengthened your ability to feel lighter for a few moments of your day. . . .

<table>
<tr><td>

STEP

EIGHT

</td><td>

Changing Powerlessness into Action

</td></tr>
</table>

Violent loss results in feelings of powerlessness, with few rights and little voice. New studies are suggesting that the act of doing something is a major path for learning to live with what has happened. Look at Appendix IV which gives examples of Heroes, Finding Meaning and Making a Difference for a small sample of what others have done.

You are not asked to do anything in this step, especially if your loss is quite recent or ongoing for some reason. You may want to wait until you are freer to put some action in place. As you can see from the examples that what one does can be of any size. What seems to matter is by doing something it moves you to replace that powerlessness.

Many folks may do something in memory of their loved one. Have any ideas come to mind for what you might want to do? We hope that we have given you examples that show that your answer of taking action is indeed personal.

We believe our loved ones are Heroes. They paid the price for trying to live in our everyday world and lost. They remind us all that we have a right to those freedoms, to move in our everyday world. Our Heroes paid the ultimate price.

In memory of Sam Knott, founder of the San Diego Crime Victims Oak Garden. From your poker buddies.

See more images in Appendix IV.

Marilyn Peterson Armour, PhD, professor at the University of Texas in Austin, has been studying survivors of homicide and finds that many do better when they engage in:

The Intense Pursuit of What Matters, such as:

- Declarations of Truth

- Expose hypocrisy

This provides a source of energy and motivation . . .

When:

- Fighting for what is right

- Living in ways that give purpose to the loved one's death

- Using experiences to benefit others

- Living life deliberately in an effort to give positive value to the homicide

This page intentionally left blank. You are encouraged to use it for writing your story or keeping notes.

STEP EIGHT, QUESTION ONE

Who do you know who has become active in a related activity after the loss of a loved one to a violent death? What action have they taken in response to a traumatic death? What examples do you have?

Remember, the names of your heroes can be those who don't get attention in the media, as the response can be any size of activity. Example: The Founder of MADD is someone who lost someone to Drunk Driving. You may have examples that you want to add to the Heroes list in Appendix IV.

Survivor Voices

STEP EIGHT, QUESTION ONE

Dee

My niece worked at a hospital in Wichita Falls, Texas. After her death in 1984, her co-workers established a fund to contribute to a wing being added to the hospital and a room would be dedicated in Tara's memory. She would have loved that.

Elena

My friend Rose lost her daughter to homicide about 20 years ago. She is our area's representative for Families and Friends of Murder Victims. Also my friend Sr. Terri lost her mother because of a drunk driver, and her brother, who was a police officer, was killed in the line of duty. She is a chaplain at the hospital now and also works with families who have lost family members to violence.

Marina

Maggie Elvey would be my choice. I got her name from Connie Saindon, who would later become my therapist for group and individual therapy. When I first spoke with Connie about two months after my father's murder, she gave me Maggie's number as a resource.

Maggie had endured the brutal murder of her husband some years earlier. Her husband lingered nearly two months in a coma before he succumbed to his injuries. His murderers were all convicted, but their sentences varied due to their ages. One is free now because he was a minor at the time of the murder. All these years later, she faithfully attends their parole hearings and keeps abreast of their activities in prison.

She also worked for Crime Victims United in Sacramento. CVUC advocates for crime victims and fights to protect our laws from being eroded by those who presumably have never suffered the

After her death in 1984, her co-workers established a fund to contribute to a wing being added to the hospital and a room would be dedicated in Tara's memory. She would have loved that.

Dee

My friend Sr. Terri lost her mother because of a drunk driver, and her brother, who was a police officer, was killed in the line of duty. She is a chaplain at the hospital now and also works with families who have lost family members to violence.

Elena

impact of violent crime. CVUC has had a pivotal role in enacting new legislation to protect survivors of violent crime, and to stiffen penalties for convicted criminals.

Frankly, I can't feature it. After seeing the criminal justice system fumble, then dump Dad's case like so much unwanted detritus, I am in awe of a person who would choose to interface with the legal system for the good of others. Where I feel contempt, bitterness and disgust, Maggie chooses to see opportunity and hope.

I'll never forget that oddly sunny August afternoon in 1999 when she took time out of her workday to hear my story and render comfort. Only a survivor of murder would know the hell I was suffering. She was the first person to give me leave to care for myself as I saw fit. She chuckled at times. I could hear the smile in her voice. I was in a sort of numb agony, if that makes sense. After spending two hours on the phone with Maggie, I nurtured a tenuous thread of hope for a future without pain, confusion, and rage.

Myra
I met Larry Edwards through my music; he has been a great help to me. I saw, through speaking to him and reading his book, that others had pain from a violent loss and that this kind of loss is very different. He has been the one person I have really met that summed up how violent loss can be difficult to deal with, and how most people don't understand it at all.

Austin
I know of others in SVLP who have engaged in SVLP activities. They have gone through the program, attended special events and memorial events, as well as becoming involved in supportive activities and SVLP.

Maggie Elvey, who works for Crime Victims United of California, would be my choice.

She was the first person to give me leave to care for myself as I saw fit. She chuckled at times. I could hear the smile in her voice. I was in a sort of numb agony, if that makes sense. After spending two hours on the phone with Maggie, I nurtured a tenuous thread of hope for a future without pain, confusion, and rage.

Marina

I was in awe of Larry Edwards, a friend, who wrote a book (Dare I Call It Murder?: A Memoir of Violent Loss).

His writing let me see that a person who wants clarity really can pursue the details if one has the patience.

Louise

Louise

I did not know any of the other people involved in the accident that killed my husband. I moved across the country and did not hear the news after that first week.

I was in awe of Larry Edwards, a friend, who wrote a book (Dare I Call It Murder?: A Memoir of Violent Loss) about the death of his parents and his efforts to unravel the circumstances. It was a major upheaval of the family; the investigation stretched across national boundaries and numerous government agencies. He also described his own group work and activities for other survivors. His writing let me see that a person who wants clarity really can pursue the details if one has the patience.

Connie

My sister's murder prompted me to find ways to help folks who had lost a loved one to murder.

As the founder of the Survivors of Violent Loss Program, I have met so many people who are true heroes to me in what they are doing in memory of their loved ones. I have reserved a special place for you to review a partial list of people who are doing activities no matter how big or small, how public or private.

Please take a look at Appendix IV—Heroes, Finding Meaning and Making a Difference.

STEP EIGHT, QUESTION TWO

What ideas do you have or might want to do to find meaning and make a difference?

Survivor Voices

Step Eight, Question Two

Dee

In 2000, the killer was found guilty in Tara's murder and sentenced to death. After the trial, I took my sister, Tara's mother, shopping to buy wind chimes. We hung them on Tara's headstone and also on or near the headstones of other family members—our grandparents, an infant nephew she never knew, and her father, who died when Tara was 14 months old. It was a good exercise for my sister and me to do together.

Later, back home, I was privileged to plant a tree at the Crime Victims Oak Garden started by another family who lost their daughter to murder. I wrote a letter to Tara and put it into the hole with the tree before filling it with dirt. That felt good.

Elena

In 2010 I was introduced to a nun who was the director for the Office of Restorative Justice in the diocese in which I live. I was interested in serving my church in some form of social justice. We discussed all the dimensions and impact violence has on a community so that I could choose in which aspect to participate. I was very drawn to grief support for families that had lost loved ones to violence.

I, along with two nuns, developed workshops to inform the community and parishes of the differences between natural and traumatic death; we developed retreats and vigils for loss to violence. Also we found this program, The Journey, which we were very drawn to because it offered a structured process to help people develop resiliencies and go from being victims to survivors to those who thrive. So I was blessed to go through this process and work to implement and offer it in our diocese.

We found this program, The Journey, which we were very drawn to because it offered a structured process to help people develop resiliencies and go from being victims to survivors to those who thrive. So I was blessed to go through this process and work to implement and offer it in our diocese.

Elena

Once in a while I am called upon to tell my story to those in the community who have suffered a traumatic loss. I have also spoken to social workers, therapists, and potential donors.

I do it because it helps me. The person who slaughtered my father went free. Unpunished. By stepping outside of my own pain and defeat, I conquer them, and prevail.

Marina

Marina

I intend to continue to support Survivors of Violent Loss by contributing funds as I am able. It is my goal to reach as many survivors of violent loss as possible so that they can receive the kind of help that I got. I used to do public speaking on behalf of SVLP, but it was very hard on me, and I decided that it wasn't the best use of my time or talents. Now I concentrate upon disseminating information on Restorative Retelling therapy. I also support the efforts of Connie Saindon, who helps find ways to train mental health clinicians in the restorative retelling model of therapy. It isn't easy to re-visit Dad's murder in order to accomplish these things. Sometimes the work is disruptive, and extremely painful.

But I do it because it helps me. The person who slaughtered my father went free. Unpunished. By stepping outside of my own pain and defeat, I conquer them, and prevail. I have dedicated my life to this precept. For example, a server at my favorite restaurant told me out of the blue that her sister had been hit and killed by a truck only three weeks before. No one really understood what had happened. It was too soon. There she was before me: numb, confused, angry, and so very alone. Was it an accident? Was it suicide? I knew she was riding what I call the "mad merry-go-round" of obsessive thought. It is a torturous ride.

Thankfully, business had reached a lull. I spoke with her for some twenty minutes. I know I said things she had never heard before. My words that were the verbal equivalent of cool, life-giving water for a human being who is dying of thirst in the desert.

I just knew. And she knew that I knew. How wonderful it was to give her my support, and the website address of Survivors of Violent Loss. When I left, she gave me a hard, impulsive hug. She knew I would come back, and that there was nothing she could say that would shock me, or drive me away.

The best part? Because of all the hard work I did individually, and in therapy, I can be a calm support to others.

I would really like to work with Veterans or at least give back to this organization, as Julian was so influenced by his time in the military, and had he reached out, I think he could have received some help.

Myra

137

This thing called violent loss can take you down, or it can enrich your life immeasurably. I choose the latter option, and helping others reminds me of that commitment.

Myra

I would really like to work with Veterans or at least give back to this organization, as Julian was so influenced by his time in the military, and had he reached out, I think he could have received some help. I haven't joined any groups. I went to one meeting for survivors and the members all seemed more dysfunctional than I was, and this was years ago. I just concentrated on healing myself and writing my own journal on the experience.

Austin

I like the "River of Remembrance" ceremony at the Oak Garden. I have assisted with a SVLP orientation, activities at the Oak Garden, and I have served on the board and as events committee chair. I am thinking of who else I can assist. I may dedicate a tree to my nephew Brad there in the Garden.

Louise

I could write or visit the courthouse where the court hearing about the accident was held somewhat later and get a copy of the proceedings.

I could go to the local newspaper(s) office and/or the Internet and read the accounts of the accident.

I could make copies of these as well as assemble copies of the photos I have, and give them to my daughter and son if they would like to know more about the death of their father.

Connie

I have found my life's mission and I plan to continue to do what this area calls upon me to do.

Now it is time to listen again to your audio CD using Step Eight, or you may read the text that follows. You may download an audio version at http://svlp.org/resources.html.

Step Eight Closing Exercise

Again . . . to get ready for this experience, sit in a comfortable chair in a quiet place where you will not be interrupted . . . then place your feet flat on the floor. . . . Sit forward and lean back with your shoulders resting on the back of your chair.

Place your hands on the upper part of your chest . . . gently, one on top of the other . . . and begin first by just noticing . . . the weight of your hands resting on your chest. . . . Make sure that your arms are not resting on the arms of the chair to get the full feel of the weight of your hands on your chest. *Now . . . notice the slight movement of your hands from your own breathing. . . .*

*Now . . . take a deep breath in through your nose and **hold it** . . . . for as long as you can . . . and when you are ready . . . form your mouth into an O . . . and slowly breath out . . . let that air go . . . all the way out. . . . Then relax . . . and . . . slump . . . keeping your hands in place . . . just slump . . . like a rag doll . . . letting those muscles go . . . and relax . . . notice how well that chair is supporting you . . . with nothing you need to do . . . no place to go . . . you can just to let go . . . and relax.*

And again continue to listen as I read this poem to you.

To Those I Love and Those Who Love Me

Author Unknown

When I am gone, release me, let me go
I have so many things to see and do.
You mustn't tie yourself to me with tears,
Be thankful for our many beautiful years.

I gave to you my love. YOU can only guess
How much you gave to me in happiness.
I thank you for the love you each have shown,
But now it's time I traveled alone.

So grieve a while for me, if grieve you must,
Then let your grief be comforted by trust.
It's only for a time that we must part,
So bless the memories within your heart.
I won't be far away, for life goes on.
So if you need me, **call** and I will come.
Though you can't see or touch me, I'll be near.
And if you listen with your heart, you'll hear
All my love around you soft and clear.

And then when you must come this way alone,
I'll greet you with a smile, and say,
"Welcome Home!"

Family & Friends

CREATING A CUSTOMIZED CEREMONY

We asked, in Step Two, who was there for you when you found out about your loved one. In this section we want to direct your attention to those who have been a support to you. They may be some family members or friends. They may be someone who is a part of your religious, work or justice community. You will be asked to meet with these people to form a ceremony or ritual that marks what you have been through together.

STEP NINE, QUESTION ONE

First, list those who have been a support to you and write about how they have been a support to you. If that has changed, describe who is there now and how they are a support to you. List those who are the most support to you now.

_____

_____

_____

_____

When you are ready, contact your supporters and ask them to join you in honoring them for the support they have given you or to mark what you have gone through together.

Rituals and Ceremonies:

- Are vehicles for respectful expression of losses

- Help to free up over-whelming emotion

- Are an aid to strengthen bonds between individuals and their community

Survivors do better with opportunities for peer support.

Early support for adults, children, and families may prevent PTSD. Once PTSD is diagnosed, it is a life-long struggle.

141

You may want to gather materials to be available for you and your support people. You may also want to read something that has been meaningful for you.

Suggestions include candles, ribbons, rope, stones, yarn, stickers, paper and pens, or balloons.

Set a specific time and time limit to do this activity. Use the article at the end of this section—"Creating a Customized Ceremony"— as an additional guide. Use the ideas here to create your own activity or create one together with your supporters. What we have found is that the rituals, the ceremonies are all different.

Survivor Voices

Step Nine, Question One

Dee

My daughter, Jessica, and my two sons, Dale and Scott, were there for me and supported me as I worked through the groups and prepared to go back to Texas for the trial. My Al-Anon friends, Kathy and Sherry, and too many others to name, were there day or night for me. They were there at weekly in meetings to listen to my pain and offered support as I tried to make sense of it all.

Elena

Any time a mass is celebrated there is an intention offered for the mass. I arranged to have mass celebrated for the intention of the life of my brother. So when it was celebrated, it was specifically for him. I, my sister, and his son were all present. Then we went out to breakfast and told stories about how he lived, not how he died.

Also, the Christmas after I took the 10-week Journey course became the first time in 19 years that I remembered my brother at Christmas. I made a Christmas tree ornament with his name on it and thanked God for him as I hung it on the tree. I felt my brother was once again alive in my life and I wanted to celebrate him. I will be doing this every Christmas.

Marina

My fiancé is my main support now. He is in law enforcement, and is also a military veteran who saw combat. He understands a lot of things about violent death that others cannot. He loves that I can tolerate his dark moments without turning away. We complement one another in that regard.

Connie Saindon is a huge help when I'm struggling with some aspect of Dad's murder. She supports me as a friend, but she knows how to

The group changed my life forever—I feel that the kind of help I received was something I only dreamed of.

The group was so different for me, other people with my exact problem. I no longer feel so alone, talking about my (son) was like a special gift.

I now feel there may be a life out there for me. But at least I feel a spark of life. There may be a place for me in this world.

Cathy, April 2001

help me attain some measure of therapeutic detachment when I'm stuck in a negative thought pattern.

Once in a while some intense emotion is aroused, and picked over in detail. But I did that so much in the beginning, with so many different people. Most of the feelings of rage, confusion, and pain that were so bitter and hard to swallow have been digested. Processed. There is little more in the way of nourishment or enlightenment to be extracted from them. Kind of like those pellets that owls expel after they've eaten some rodent. The useful parts are absorbed, leaving only the skin, hair, and bones behind, in a neatly packaged little ball.

The harsh reality is that for the rest of my days, memories of the murder will surface at unexpected times, and in novel ways. Once in a while I recognize the need to surrender to them entirely, until the storm in my mind passes. Most of the time I use the power of what I learned in cognitive therapy to turn to more productive thoughts.

Seeking out to my fellow survivors for support is another option. They will always understand. That way I don't burden my loved ones, who have had to endure this with me for so very long.

Austin

At this time I do not feel a need to conduct another ceremony. Perhaps in the future. I went to Brad's memorial service, and my niece and I, along with others, did a sort of memorial at last year's River of Remembrance event at the Oak Garden. In 2006, I also made a Christmas ornament for Brad for the Christmas Memorial event. I was out of town for the event in 2007. I feel this is enough for now. I think it is time to remember Brad as a beautiful soul. For me, ceremonies are not something I feel a need for. I am a very "interior" person and don't feel comfortable in outward demonstrations.

Louise

My father was very supportive. He flew to us and drove me and the children to my husband's state, then on to California. He took care of all the correspondence with the company and insurance company while settlements were being made. He gave me advice about applying to college, moving, and getting a routine established for going to school and taking care of life in general. My husband's parents were very supportive, visiting us and making us welcome while visiting them. They were a continuing part of their grandchildren's lives.

Connie

Support continues to grow nationally as well as in the community that I reside. One ritual that I have developed is to have everyone hang a symbol at the same time we are doing our holiday memorial in December. We send out email blasts and invite everyone to join us in acknowledging our common bond and support for one another. One dear sister that has been a great and continuing support waits for the announcement so she can hang her ornament, her symbol of our sister, at the same time.

Creating a Customized Ceremony

In developing your ceremony, consider including several nonverbal actions and symbolic activities. The following are suggestions for you:

Reading of names

Forming a circle

Reading a poem or verse that is special for you

Cross from one place to another

Naming the traumatic experience

Chanting

Call and response from leader to "chorus"

Symbols of overcoming: lifting up, rising, opening

Moving in a circle

Cutting a ribbon, rope

Repeating phrases

Symbols of burdens, obstacles, barriers

Lighting a candle

Planting bulbs

Washing hands

Rolling/throwing a ball of yarn from one to another until all in the circle are connected

This page intentionally left blank. You are encouraged to use it for writing your story or keeping notes.

STEP NINE, QUESTION TWO

Complete this section by describing what rituals or ceremonies you have come up with. You may already have some that you are doing. If so, describe what you do as well.

Survivor Voices

STEP NINE, QUESTION TWO

Dee
The rituals done in the Survivors' Groups were very special. Tokens were selected, used, and shared in a special way to pay tribute to our lost loved ones. These rituals created many different feelings, emotions and ties to all the participants. It bonded us in a very special and meaningful way.

Now I light candles on Tara's birthday and the anniversary of her death. The glow gives me a sense of her presence. I reflect on her life and her positive influence she has had on my life and the lives of my children and family, some born long since her death, but who know her.

Elena
I have a little plastic tube I keep with me which reminds me of Phillip drinking beer out of my sister's fish filter. I shared it with her and we both had a great laugh. I gave her one and she now carries it as well.

Marina
I had a few spontaneous little ceremonies that I performed. When I went trekking in the Himalayas the year after the murder, I made it a point to have a Buddhist friend take me to some temples and monasteries to make offerings in Dad's name. While I am an atheist, I believe there is comfort in a ceremony that evolved to acknowledge the dead. The monasteries are very peaceful, and quite ancient. Buddhism stresses the transitory nature of life, and there are many symbols that convey that message. Beautiful things, everywhere one looks . . . objects darkened and mellowed with age. Changed.

I cannot help but be struck by the fact that life is so brief and unimportant before the immense

Family and friends created a ceremonial tree.

I light candles on Tara's birthday and the anniversary of her death. The glow gives me a sense of her presence.

Dee

I have a little plastic tube I keep with me that reminds me of Phillip drinking beer out of my sister's fish filter.

Elena

When I went trekking in the Himalayas the year after the murder, I made it a point to have a Buddhist friend take me to some temples and monasteries to make offerings in Dad's name.

Marina

span of time. It's really pretty invigorating, and joyous. I have been back several times since, and always do the same thing.

I also bought colorful Buddhist prayer flags. I brought them home and strung them on the fence above my house. They flutter quite prettily in the wind. Buddhists believe that the prayers printed upon them are somehow repeated or recited every time the flags flap. I don't really believe this, but it's a nice thought, and a nice way to acknowledge my father's life—and death.

Myra

At the end of the second year, on my husband's anniversary, his dearest friends and I put his ashes (those that didn't make it into the wall) into the ocean. We ate all of his favorite foods and had a lot of cocktails in his honor. This was one step in my closure process. I also placed his ashes into the waters off Alaska, where he had lived and where he always wanted to return. I still have some of his ashes, and if I can ever get to Vietnam, I will place some there, too.

Austin

I went to Brad's memorial service and my niece and I, along with others, did a sort of memorial at last year's River of Remembrance event at the Oak Garden. In 2006, I also made a Christmas ornament for Brad for the Christmas Memorial event. I was out of town for the event in 2007. I feel this is enough for now. I think it is time to remember Brad as a beautiful soul. For me, ceremonies are not something I feel a need for. I am a very "interior" person and don't feel comfortable in outward demonstrations.

His dearest friends and I put his ashes into the ocean. We ate all of his favorite foods and had a lot of cocktails in his honor.

Myra

I always pause and remember my husband on August 9th.

In the future I could mention the significance of the date to my sister and brother and my children so they could remember with me for a moment. That might make me feel less alone with it.

Louise

A ritual that I created and conducted with my family is a photo album along with the stories. We called it our living memory of her. It is still a precious album for us all.

Connie

Louise
I do not feel the urge to create a ritual for myself or others. I always pause and remember my husband on August 9th. I haven't been in the habit of discussing the date or events with anyone.

In the future I could mention the significance of the date to my sister and brother and my children so they could remember with me for a moment. That might make me feel less alone with it.

Connie
A ritual that I created and conducted with my family is: I collected all the photos from aunts, cousins, siblings, and parents of "Tiny." This was before the era of digital scanning and cameras. So, the task was to take the "borrowed" photo to a photo developer and have them photograph the photo and make a negative and a replacement photo for me to use to add to this collection. I then returned the photo to the family member who loaned it to me. Then, at different times, I sat with my immediate family and had them select the photos that they wanted to use to create a page in a photo album along with the stories that they wrote on the page itself. We called it our living memory of her. It is still a precious album for us all.

Now it is time to listen again to your audio CD using Step Nine, or you may read the text that follows. You may download an audio version at http://svlp.org/resources.html.

Step Nine Closing Exercise

Again . . . to get ready for this experience, sit in a comfortable chair in a quiet place where you will not be interrupted . . . then place your feet flat on the floor. . . . Sit forward and lean back with your shoulders resting on the back of your chair.

Place your hands on the upper part of your chest . . . gently, one on top of the other . . . and begin first by just noticing . . . the weight of your hands resting on your chest. . . . Make sure that your arms are not resting on the arms of the chair to get the full feel of the weight of your hands on your chest. Now . . . notice the slight movement of your hands from your own breathing. . . .

You may find that closing your eyes helps you to focus more on these slight sensations. Again . . . notice the slight movement of your hands from your own breathing. . . . You may also notice your heartbeat. . . . Just notice this for a few moments. Notice the rise and fall of your chest from your own breathing.

Now . . . take a deep breath in through your nose and **hold it** *. . . . . for as long as you can . . . and when you are ready . . . form your mouth into an O . . . and slowly breath out . . . let that air go . . . all the way out. . . . Then relax . . . and . . . slump . . . keeping your hands in place . . . just slump . . . like a rag doll . . . letting those muscles go . . . and relax . . . notice how well that chair is supporting you . . . with nothing you need to do . . . no place to go . . . you can just to let go . . . and relax.*

And . . . continue your relaxed breathing and listen as I read the words of poem that I would like you to hear.

Don't Quit

Author Unknown
(Submitted by Sharon Mont's mom, Darlene Bevers)

When things go wrong, as they
sometimes will,
When the road you're trudging seems
All uphill,
When the funds are low and the
Debts are high,
And you want to smile, but you have
To sigh,
When care is pressing you down a
bit—
Rest if you must, but don't you quit.

Life is queer with its twists and turns,
As every one of us sometimes learns,
And many a fellow turns about
When he might have won had he
stuck it out.
Don't give up though the pace seems
slow—
You may succeed with another blow.

Often the goal is nearer than
It seems to a faint and faltering man;
Often the struggler has given up
When he might have captured the
victor's cup;
And he learned too late when the
night came down,
How close he was to the golden
crown.

Success is failure turned inside out—
The silver tint of the clouds of doubt,
And you never can tell how close you
are,
It may be near when it seems afar;
So stick to the fight when you're
hardest hit—
It's when things seem worst that you
mustn't quit.

When you are ready . . . take your time . . . and notice the room you are in . . . and slowly resume your day. . . .

Re-Member-ing

The final step in this workbook for you should not be misunderstood as the final step in your Journey. We know that what has happened to you is a life-long process. We also do not think that you are indeed "over it" in these ten steps that you have shared with leaders in this specialized field of violent-death loss and with other survivors.

What we do know is that going through these steps helps to shore up your natural abilities to help you accommodate your loss, and to help you not feel so very alone.

We hope this process will help you fend off folks who are well-meaning but misinformed. You won't get over it. Normal has now changed forever. Most reactions are **normal** for this *abnormal* event that has happened to you.

With that being said, this step is to add another layer to help you buffer your loss. In the previous step, we encouraged taking action. In this step, we put in place another way to help remember your loved one.

Many survivors have told us they worry their loved ones will be forgotten. Old ideas about grief and loss had to do with severing ties with those who died. It was thought this would help reduce the

The empirical reality is that people do not relinquish their ties to the deceased . . . or let them go. What occurs is a transformation of their relationship into more symbolic and inter- nalized and often more elaborate forms.
    Zisook and Shuchter, 1993

The possibility of a continued relationship with the deceased is well accepted in many cultures. An example is the Mexican annual event of the "Day of the Dead."

Summoning the Deceased, what would they want?

This can aid the family bond as well, with considerations such as:

They would want us

- To go on

- To remember them

- To celebrate what a great life they had

suffering of the bereaved. This process had the impact of dis-member-ing our loved ones from our families. New understanding has us look at how our loved ones are still with us after death and the importance of re-member-ing them. After death, they are still in our lives in various ways.

You are now asked to come up with a symbol, not one your family may have come up with, but your very own personal symbol of your loved one.

What are your ideas? What would symbolize your loved one's life? Find a way to ensure it has physical properties even if it is a photo copy. You want it to be something that you can replicate so you can give it to others to help them remember your loved one as well. They may have ideas for their memento as well.

Once you have done this, give your item to anyone you want to help remember them. Let friends and family and other supporters know why you selected the item that you did, what meaning it has for you. If you are in a support group, you may ask group members to bring symbols of their loved ones. Ask them to bring one for each person. If there are five of you, ask them to bring five of them. The symbol can be as simple as a sticker, a candle, a pencil with angels on it, a copy of a sketch someone has done, a rubber band, and so on. It is important that the symbol has physical properties.

Step Ten, Question One

Together we carry the burden of what happened to our loved ones, and we honor them by remembering what their lives were like. Mementos, or symbols, help us remember them.

What symbol would be a memento of your loved one's life? What symbols do others have for this person? List them here. Also, look at what the Survivor Writers tell you about their mementos listed later in this section of the workbook.

Mosaic: Collection of Symbols

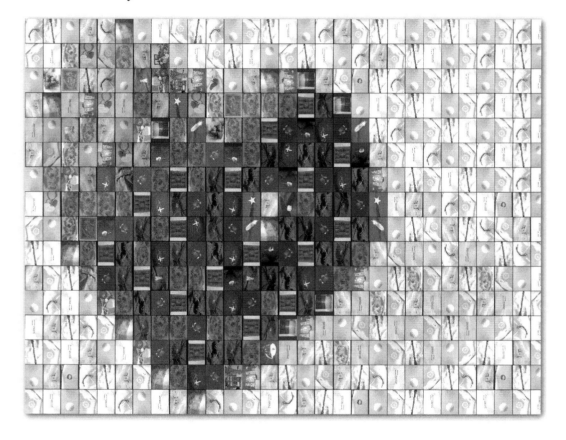

Survivor Voices

STEP TEN, QUESTION ONE

Dee

Tara had so many interests. She loved rainbows and unicorns. My memento for her is the picture on the Christmas card she mailed to me on the day she was killed, December 21, 1984. I received the card in the mail on Christmas Eve. It had a picture of three unicorns in the clouds with a beautiful rainbow behind them. I laminated that page and on the reverse side I put a phrase from my "Courage to Change" book that said, "God gave us memories so that we might have roses in December," by James M. Barrie.

Elena

He was a classic surfer California kid. His first action every morning was to look for the sun.

My favorite memory of Phillip will always be of him in search of the sun, as the sunflower does :)

Sunflowers remind me of my brother because they personify who he was and what he loved, being in the sun and rejoicing in its warmth. When I see them, I remember him at his best and it brings me joy.

Marina

I chose a tail feather from my late Amazon parrot, Gideon, as my symbol. Gideon was a Christmas gift from my father. It was 1969, and I was ten years old. I still remember the thrill of coming into the den and seeing a cage with a big red bow on it next to the Christmas tree.

This is a hard question to answer, because my father was a complicated man. He lived a full and varied life. So many things symbolize his life.

But after much reflection, I've decided that the desert symbolizes his life. He loved the desert, and spent a good portion of his life there. He found

> *He was a classic surfer California kid. His first action every morning was to look for the sun.*
>
> *My favorite memory of Phillip will always be of him in search of the sun, as the sunflower does :)*
>
> Elena

> *I've decided that the desert symbolizes his life. He loved the desert, and spent a good portion of his life there. He found freedom there, and beauty.*
>
> Marina

freedom there, and beauty. He was also murdered there.

He spent a lot of time in Baja California. A friend took him there in the late '60s. He was starting his company at the time. Life was very stressful for him. He found peace and relaxation on his visits to the Forgotten Peninsula.

He couldn't stop talking about it after his first trip. Within a year, he took me on a trip there. I fell immediately and profoundly in love. I was only ten years old, but my imagination was fully captured by this wild and breathtaking place. It was so different from the coastal California town where I grew up, but the ocean was there, just like at home. I've always felt at ease in the ocean, but this one was so clear and warm, and bursting with life.

Six years later, Dad proudly bought a home in the Coachella Valley. He moved once, but he never left the desert.

He loved the heat of the summer, and the calm, cool, starry nights of winter. He enjoyed pointing out the contrast between the flourishing palm trees, and the snow-covered mountains that framed them for several months of the year. He admired the tenacity and resourcefulness of the plants and animals that thrived in its apparent wastes.

Maybe he even identified with those things, just a little.

When he was murdered there, it was almost unbearable. I wondered if my love of the desert would be compromised forever. I really, really worked hard to embrace his life and death so that it would not happen. I remember the banner day, four years after the murder, when I gazed upon his beloved home from the mountains far above, and saw only my beloved desert once more. Triumph. Yet it took more years of hard work to truly recapture all of the joy I felt before the murder.

For many years of my own life, I have made it a special mission to travel the world's great deserts.

I have kept mementos of his life, his special camping tools, his movie books, and his old book collection.

Myra

The things that help me remember are some pieces of wood furniture that my husband made.

Louise

The symbol I have selected is the iris . . . a symbol for Hope.

Connie

I have walked in the Sahara and the Namib, the Gobi, and the Rub' al Khali. Someday I will journey to the Atacama, the Taklimakan, and the Great Sandy Desert. I'm not looking for anything. I just love the peace, and the vast, empty spaces, where one can be alone with one's thoughts, and with one's self.

And I will always, always, remember Dad when I go there. I am forever grateful that he shared his great love of the desert with me.

Myra

I have kept mementos of his life, his special camping tools, his movie books, and his old book collection. My house is filled with his mementos as he redesigned most of the house. I plan to follow his plan for the garden when I have the money, since he had amazing insight and I feel it would be in his honor. The icon is a mosaic he created for our patio.

Austin

Someone wrote a song for Brad and recorded it. I had a rock engraved with his name and placed it in the River of Remembrance at the Oak Garden.

Louise

The things that help me remember are some pieces of wood furniture that my husband made. I have two lamps and a chest with shelves that hold my record player and records—some of which we shared when we first met. I also have some of the household items that were wedding presents to us or that I bought at the time we married. In addition, I have photographs. Some are in my digital picture frame, and they flip by, along with other photos of family, friends, and events that make me happy.

My daughter has photographs of her Dad and grandparents in her home, along with the desk he made.

My son has the extra-long, twin-bed frame he made and my grandson sleeps in it every night.

Connie

The symbol I have selected is the iris. I think the iris reminded me of my sister and her lavender dress that she wore at my wedding. It also reminded me of her as there is a native iris that grows in our swampland areas and she loved the flowers that grew in our woods. I didn't know it when I selected it, but the iris is also a symbol for Hope. It is quite fitting to be my symbol for Tiny. I have received wonderful gifts and have quite a collection of photos of irises as well. The symbol you see here is made from tissue paper and is a gift from two related families that grew much closer together after working with our program and then becoming volunteers to help others. So when you see an iris, wild or not, please help me remember my sister.

STEP TEN, QUESTION TWO

How are you doing now? We have taken you on a journey, one of many you will take, but this one has ten steps in this workbook. We have included voices from others, as well as examples from other survivors.

We want to know, how you are doing now? Please note here the changes you have made going through these ten steps.

What is better? What struggles continue?

Have you listened to the audio recordings?

Have you been able to call upon the calming skills at other times as well?

Note what is working and what resources you still want more of.

Survivor Voices

STEP TEN, QUESTION TWO

Dee
Since the group, and working these questions, my life has been enriched with the friendships of those who made this journey with me. I continue to give back to the groups as much as I can. What I have learned has helped me cope with subsequent losses in my life. It has helped me to be a better support to friends, family members and extended family members and friends when they experience a death in their lives. When my children's stepbrother, Vincent Thomas, was murdered in 2001, I told my ex-husband, Bob, and his wife, Jo Jo, about the Survivors group. This helped both of them and other members of Jo Jo's family as they went through the group. But most remarkably, it forged a friendship between me and Jo Jo. It has facilitated healing between me, Bob, and Jo Jo. This in turn has changed everything for my children. We now parent and support our children collectively. We celebrate holidays and birthdays together. We have planned and celebrated weddings on both sides together. Celebrated the births of grandchildren on both sides and offered support after deaths on both sides of each other's families. I've been let into the lives of my children's extended family and now we call each other family. Dark Miracles, Jo Jo calls them.

Elena
It had been 19 years since my brother died when I took this "Journey." My intention in doing so was only to audit the program so that I would not be asking others to do something I myself was not willing to do. I did not think that there was still undiscovered pain and grief in need of healing.

The greatest change (and it's a big one) is that I have let go of my unconscious resentment and anger toward my brother, and I can remember him again joyfully. The memory of how he died

My life has been enriched with the friendships of those who made this journey with me.

Dee

The greatest change (and it's a big one) is that I have let go of my unconscious resentment and anger toward my brother, and I can remember him again joyfully.

Elena

Milena (Sellers) Phillips co-authored *Always Fly Away* so her son's death would not be in vain. The book help in teaching children how to stay safe from predators.

does not surface in the old way, but the image of me loving him does, and that gives me peace. In spiritual terms, my brother and I are living a Resurrection.

Marina

How am I doing now? Sixteen years after Dad's murder, I'm doing pretty well. That I just wrote the preceding sentence without feeling sad is quite amazing, in and of itself. Not to say that there aren't dark moments, even now. There always will be triggers. Murder trial coverage is one. I still feel bitter envy when I see a murderer convicted by a jury. There is a light overlay of joy for the survivors, but their truth is not my truth, so the bitterness wins. So be it. I have trained myself not to dwell upon such things for more than a few minutes. Then I redirect my thoughts. I call it "changing the channel." I make myself forget, through sheer force of will. By going on to something else, I choose life instead of death.

For too long after the murder, and the failed trial, pain marked the days and nights of my life. I felt I was doomed to a colorless, half-waking existence. I thought, "What the hell am I supposed to do now? What is my purpose from here on out? How do I create something out of what feels like nothing? How do I make life relevant again, especially when nothing seems to matter anymore?"

I'm not going to pull any punches here. There were some things about being a victim-survivor of murder that I had gotten a little too used to: The attention. The sympathy. The sense that I could somehow avoid the effort of being a sentient, involved human being. Being out in the world was sometimes just a little too much trouble. Why not stay in the limbo of eternal victimhood forever? It was a tempting path, but it was a path of decay, of inner rot. Deep down I knew it.

Murder had defined and ordered the days of my life for too long. I didn't want the balance of my existence forever defined by a single act of terrible violence.

How am I doing now? Sixteen years after Dad's murder, I'm doing pretty well. That I just wrote the preceding sentence without feeling sad is quite amazing, in and of itself.

Murder had defined and ordered the days of my life for too long. I didn't want the balance of my existence forever defined by a single act of terrible violence.

Yes, I wish I didn't know how easy it is to die. I wish I didn't know how close death walks to each and every one of us, every moment of the day.

It helps keep me out of trouble.

It makes me thankful for my good health, my loved ones, my beautiful life. And I'm not going back.

Marina

To paraphrase the thoughts of a traumatized character in the Steven King book "From a Buick Eight," I decided I wanted to be refined by tragedy rather than defined by it. That remains my goal today. I'll never "get over" Dad's murder. It will forever inform my life, whether I am aware of it or not. It is like a subterranean river that flows dark and unseen. But in a strange way, it enriches my days. I paid dearly for my knowledge of life, and of human nature. I sure know myself a whole lot better. Imagine life as a map: I've got a better one now.

Yes, I wish I didn't know how easy it is to die. I wish I didn't know how close death walks to each and every one of us, every moment of the day. I wish I could walk around blissfully ignorant of life's horrors. But you know what? Life is pretty damned good after all of these years. I use my experience of violent death to live in gratitude every day. It helps keep me out of trouble. It helps keep me away from the bad people, the toxic people, the emotional parasites. It makes me thankful for my good health, my loved ones, my beautiful life. And I'm not going back.

 **Myra**

I am doing well now. I have my moments; it is to be expected. I still can't hear sirens go by the house without a little lump in my throat. I try not to dwell on his passing as much as the good times we shared. It has been a long road to learn that I didn't cause his suicide. That he had choices and I couldn't make them for him, and that he is now in a more peaceful place.

I am thankful for the years we had and wish he were still here, but know that now I have other friends to fill that void. I have made new male relationships that bring me peace and joy, something I never thought could happen. I am stronger than I was, and know that life can change in a minute and that you have to be ready to change with it. I am lucky to have such an amazing support system and lucky that what Hospice told me to do really did work for me.

I am doing well now. I have my moments; it is to be expected. I still can't hear sirens go by the house without a little lump in my throat.

Myra

I like this journey and the steps it has taken me on. It has been helpful and a comfortable one—full of fond memories and "deeds well done." Thank you for creating the Journey Steps.

Austin

My spiritual beliefs in the continuance of the spirit/soul and the potential for cross-boundary communication have been fortified through the years. I believe he and I may end up together in another lifetime in some capacity.

Louise

Austin

I am doing well. This Journey has given me an opportunity to review events connected to Brad's death and look upon them from a distance. I can see that I am comfortable with his "going on" and my part in supporting others. Their pain is not gone and may never go away, but mine has and I am at peace. I like this journey and the steps it has taken me on. It has been helpful and a comfortable one—full of fond memories and "deeds well done." Thank you for creating the Journey Steps.

I did not listen to the audio tape. I did not feel a need to but will listen to some now.

Louise

I'm doing well. Fifty years has created perspective. Other "life" has affected me in the interim. My spiritual beliefs in the continuance of the spirit/soul and the potential for cross-boundary communication have been fortified through the years. I believe he and I may end up together in another lifetime in some capacity. The belief that he still loves me and the memory of our life together is a good part of my life. At times I still wonder in what subtle ways it has affected my children to grow up without their father, and if/how it might have affected my own ability/willingness to commit to another partner in marriage.

Connie

I have been privileged to be with many of you on your journey and know you have joined me on mine as well. I have seen such strengths in you along with great pain. Only by going through the steps in the workbook can I also be with so many stories, so many tragedies. I hope that I have been a part of your living better with what has happened and you can continue to be a source of strength for others. I worry that many are not informed of this book and cannot benefit from the steps in this book. We have found that people in our actual groups, that this work is adapted from, have made significant improvements in their ability to live with what has happened. I am greatly indebted to Dr. Rynearson, whose work has inspired this book and for all of you who continue to let me know that what we are doing is truly making a difference for you and your families. My hope is that more folks will benefit from this work, and hopefully stave off more serious problems with their health and well-being and isolation.

Now it is time to listen again to your audio CD using Step Six, or you may read the text that follows. You may download an audio version at http://svlp.org/resources.html.

Remember, you have been building your ability to manage your emotional state by quieting yourself and using this simple yet powerful quieting strategy. It will be similar to other activities you may do or are familiar with, such as breathing techniques you do in yoga, meditation, Lamaze and so on.

This is the time to review where you have been and how far you have come. Take a look at the additional resources provided for you in Appendix II (books and links) in this workbook. You are the specialist in your story, and you may want to add to your understanding by further study with some of these resources.

Step Ten Closing Exercise

To get ready for this experience, sit in a comfortable chair in a quiet place where you will not be interrupted . . . then place your feet flat on the floor. . . . Sit forward and lean back with your shoulders resting on the back of your chair. You may discover that you are sitting in a slant with your buttocks closer to the edge of your chair leaning back. (You may also lie down to do this.)

Place your hands on the upper part of your chest . . . gently, one on top of the other . . . and begin first by just noticing . . . the weight of your hands resting on your chest. . . . Make sure that your arms are not resting on the arms of the chair to get the full feel of the weight of your hands on your chest. . . . Now . . . notice the slight movement of your hands from your own breathing. . . .

You may find that closing your eyes helps you to focus more on these slight sensations. Again . . . notice the slight movement of your hands from your own breathing. . . . You may also notice your heartbeat. . . . Just notice this for a few moments. . . . Make sure that your elbows are not resting on the chair, that they are free. . . . Notice, again, the weight of your hands on your chest . . . resting gently. Notice the rise and fall of your chest from your own breathing.

*Now . . . take a deep breath in through your nose and **hold it** . . . . for as long as you can . . . and when you are ready . . . form your mouth into an O . . . and slowly breath out . . . let that air go . . . all the way out. . . . Then relax . . . and . . . slump . . . keeping your hands in place . . . just slump . . . like a rag doll . . . letting those muscles go . . . and relax . . . notice how well that chair is supporting you . . . with nothing you need to do . . . no place to go . . . you can just to let go . . . and relax.*

And again, continue taking periodic deep breaths after normal breaths as I read this poem to you. . . . Or read the poem that follows.

When You Love Someone

Author Unknown

When you love someone, they're never far away,
Because they're always with you.
That's because love has no time or space.
It just continues on forever.
I will see you in the falling snow.
I will see you where the green grass grows.
I will hear you when I listen.
Wherever the soft wind blows.
I will see you in the northern lights.
I will see you in every star.
I will see you wherever I wander,
No matter how far.
I will keep listening and I will keep looking
And I will keep remembering
Long after the days are gone.
For our love will always live on.

Take your time to come back to the experience of being in the room . . . to your day . . .
knowing you have strengthened your ability to feel lighter for a few moments of your day. . . .

Appendix I

Survivor Voices

We find remarkable resilience in everyone we work with. We continue to be amazed at what resources people have and can draw upon. Although wounded and changed forever by what has happened, they persevere and in time find ways to rebuild their lives. It is hoped that through their painful stories you will find inspiration for your own journey.

You can read about the meanings of the mementos/symbols the Survivor Writers chose to represent their loved ones beginning on page 160, in Step Ten.

 **Dee**, Survivors Club leader
Lost her niece, Tara, a young nursing student, who was murdered. Tara's death remained unsolved for more than thirteen years. It is now known that she was the first of five in a serial killing spree.

 **Elena**, nurse, support group facilitator
Lost her adult brother to suicide.

 **Marina**, major donor for crime victims
Her father's alleged killer was prosecuted, but it ended in a mistrial and was not retried.

 **Myra**, a school teacher and musician
Lost her husband to suicide.

 **Austin**, volunteer with violent loss survivors
Lost his nephew, who was working as a photojournalist in Oaxaca, Mexico, in 2007.

continued on page 168

continued from page 167

 **Louise**, dietitian, author, and public speaker
Lost her husband in a catastrophic workplace accident.

 **Connie Saindon**, author, researcher, and founder of the Survivors of Violent Loss Program
Lost her 17-year-old sister Tiny in 1961 in a small New England town.

Appendix II

Resources

Books for Survivors
Internet Links

Books for Survivors of Violent Loss

Murder Survivor's Handbook: Real-Life Stories, Tips & Resources. Saindon, Connie (2014). Wigeon Publishing, San Diego, CA.

Dare I Call It Murder?: A Memoir of Violent Loss. Edwards, Larry M. (2013). Wigeon Publishing, San Diego, CA.

Retelling Violent Death. Rynearson, E. (2001). Brunner-Routledge, New York, NY.

No Time for Goodbyes: Coping with Sorrow, Anger and Injustice After a Tragic Death. Lord, Janice (1991). Pathfinder Publisher, Ventura, CA.

And I Don't Want to Live This Life: A Mother's Story of Her Daughter's Murder. Spungen, Deborah (1983). Villard Books, New York, NY.

What to Do When the Police Leave: A Guide to the First Days of Traumatic Aftermath. Jenkins, Bill (2001). WJB Press, Richmond, VA.

Down Range: To Iraq and Back. Cantrell, Dean, Bridget C. and Chuck (2005). Hearts Toward Home International, Bellingham, WA.

Coping with the Sudden Death of Your Loved One: A Self-help Handbook for Traumatic Bereavement. Rando, Therese. (In Press) Dog Ear Publishing, Indianapolis, IN.

Living with Grief after Sudden Loss: Suicide, Homicide, Accident, Heart Attack, Stroke. Doka, Kenneth, Editor (1996). Taylor & Francis, Bristol, PA.

Scream at the Sky: Five Texas Murders and One Man's Crusade for Justice. Stowers, Carlton (2003). St. Martin's Press, New York, NY.

Shattered Assumptions: Towards a New Psychology of Trauma. Janoff-Bulman, R. (1992) The Free Press, New York, NY.

Too Scared to Cry. Terr, Lenore (1990). Harper and Row, New York, NY.

The Resilient Self: How Survivors of Troubled Families Rise Above Adversity. Wolin, S., & Wolin, S. (1993). Villard Books, New York, NY.

Transcending: Reflections of Crime Victims. Zehr, Howard (2001). Good Books, Intercourse, PA.

All the Wrong Places. Conners, Philip (2015). W.W.Norton Publishing Co., New York, NY.

Against Terrible Odds: Lessons in resilience from Our Children. Levin, Saul, & Heather Wood Ion (2002). Bull Publishing Company, Boulder, CO.

Thanks For Asking: A Collection of Remembrances by Parents of Murdered Children & Other Survivors of Homicide Victims (1991). Printed and distributed by Parents of Murdered Children, Inc., Cincinnati, OH.

I Can't Get Over It: A Handbook for Trauma Survivors. Matsakis, Aphrodite, PhD (1992). New Harbinger Publications, Inc., Oakland, CA.

Man's Search for Meaning. Frankl, Victor (1984). Simon & Schuster, New York, NY.

Harsh Grief, Gentle Hope. White, Mary A. (1995) NavPress Publishing Group, Carol Stream, IL.

Children Mourning, Mourning Children. Doka, Kenneth, Editor (1995). Hospice Foundation of America, Taylor & Francis Publishers, New York, NY.

Point of Fracture: Voices of Heinous Crime Survivors. Zuckerman, Amy & Nystedt, Karen (1998). Zuckerman, Tucson, AZ.

Internet Links

Survivors of Violent Loss Program

 http://www.svlp.org
 blog: https://svlnetwork.wordpress.com/

Murder Survivor's Handbook

 http://wigeonpublishing.com/books/murder_survivors_handbook_saindon.html
 Facebook: https://www.facebook.com/homicidesurvivorshandbook

Hope Gallery

 https://hopegallery.smugmug.com/

Violent Death Bereavement Society

 http://www.vdbs.org

NOVA: The National Organization for Victim Assistance

 http://www.trynova.org

National Center for Victims of Crime

 https://www.victimsofcrime.org/

Parents of Murdered Children, Inc.

 www.pomc.com

Citizens Against Homicide

 http://www.citizensagainsthomicide.org

American Association of Suicidology

 http://www.suicidology.org

Survivors of Suicide

 http://www.survivorsofsuicide.com

Gift from Within

 An International Organization for Survivors of Trauma and Victimization
 http://www.giftfromwithin.org

MADD — Mothers Against Drunk Driving
   http://www.madd.org

Crime Victims United of California
   http://www.crimevictimsunited.com

Bereavement Magazine, a Magazine of Hope and Healing
   http://www.bereavementmag.com

Compassionate Friends
   http://compassionatefriends.org

Student Guidebook **by Dr. Steve Schlozman,** associate director of The Clay Center
   for Young Healthy Minds and assistant professor of psychiatry at Harvard Medical
   School, and A. Michele Tedder, founder and CEO of Joy for Life
   http://www.learnpsychology.org/suicide-depression-student-guidebook/

Appendix III

Poems

The "Changed Forever"
Butterfly: A Star Is Reborn
In the Middle of the Night

What Gift Can You Give Yourself?

Coping with Life's Blows

Make the Most of Today

Stories

Dawn V.
Clara Rose
Chuck's Story: Unsolved
I Wish Angelena Could Have Known Her Daddy

Reactions

I Know How You Feel . . .
Walk in My Shoes . . .

More Voices

The Homicide Diet

The "Changed Forever"

As I walk through the shadows of death,
and I now know evil.
I refuse to let the shadow of evil keep me from appreciating life,
the newness and joys available every day.

Whether that be seeing a new mural in a small town
or noticing dried leaves blown into a bouquet by the wind;
seeing the drops of water on an unopened bud,
the smile on the faces I pass.

As I walk through the shadows of death,
and I now know evil.
I refuse to let evil keep me from appreciating life,
the newness and joys available every day.

Smelling the pine-filled breeze in the forest,
tasting a slice of foot-high lemon meringue pie found off the Illinois I-40,
or noticing the strengths in people
who also know evil, as they have lost love ones to murder.

They too are the "changed forever."
I refuse to let the shadow of evil keep me from seeing their strengths
amid their raw devastation,
or honoring their work, making a difference for
those "changed forever."

As I walk through the shadows of death,
and I now know evil. I am not lost.

Connie Saindon (2013)

Butterfly: A Star Is Reborn

Music and lyrics by Gary Christopher Tumolo, 1998

Now you have gone
Far away from this world of ours
Now you are one with the moon and the stars
You deeply touched
Touched my heart with the sweetest song
You gave so much
All the time, all along

Like a butterfly
Out from your cocoon
Straight up to the sky
Beside the moon

Spread your wings and fly
To where you wanna be
You're a butterfly
Flying high, flying proud, flying free

Ev'ry time a star falls from the sky,
Somewhere, the star's re-born
Ev'ry time the sun sets into night
It rises into dawn
Though you may grieve, please do believe
The truth, that life lives on
Ev'ry time a star falls from the sky,
Somewhere, the star is re-born

The caterpillar in its cocoon
Surely doesn't die
One bright morn it is transformed
Into the butterfly

I will light a candle for your soul,
With love, to light the way
The memories I'll keep alive
Inside my heart they'll stay
I will say good-bye and wave on high
As your journey moves you on
Anytime a star falls from the sky,
Somewhere, the star is re-born
a butterfly

continued on page 176

continued from page 175

Out from your cocoon
Straight up to the sky
Beside the moon

Spread your wings and fly
To where you wanna be
You're a butterfly
Flying high, flying proud, flying free
You can go anywhere
Good-bye, butterfly
Flying high, flying proud, flying free!

In the Middle of the Night

Every morning when I wake
Every evening before I close my eyes
And all the in-between times
My thoughts dwell on you.
I imagine the horror of your
Last moments
Those moments won't leave me be.

In the middle of the night
Are my worst times.
In my mind I hold you close and
Say love things
I see you as you were in your
Young manhood—
Handsome, tall, smile with no end.
I see you playing baseball—
Your greatest love
I see you playing with your nephew
You loved being asked—"Is he yours?
He looks just like you"
I hear you saying "Hey, old lady"
To me when you walked in the door.

In the middle of the night
Are my worst times.
Never to see you again
Never to hear you again
Most of all—never to hug
And kiss you again
This is more than I can bear.
I touch some of your things
To feel close to you
And repeat "I love you"
Again and again.
Son of mine—I love you.

In the middle of the night
Are my worst times.

Your Grieving Mom

What Gift Can You Give Yourself?

What gift can you give yourself? Live the best life you can—every day a new beginning. You are still alive, for better or worse, and have the greatest of the human freedoms, the freedom to choose how you will live.

There is still time for you to live, time for you to enjoy—time to build yourself a good life, one that honors and embraces, rather than only mourns your loved one or is embittered by the traumatic experience you have been through.

The Jewish prayer for Yom Kippur says it best:

> It is hard to sing of oneness when our world is not complete, when those who once brought wholeness to our life have gone and nothing but memory can fill the emptiness their passing leaves behind.

> But memory can tell us only what we were, in company with those we loved; it cannot help us find what each of us, alone, must now become. Yet no one is really alone: those who live no more echo still within our thoughts and words, and what they did is part of what we have become.

> We do best homage to our dead when we live our lives most fully, even in the shadow of our loss.

Kathleen O'Hara
A Grief Like No Other (2006)
(used with permission)

Coping with Life's Blows by Being "Adopted" by Nature

by Connie Saindon

One day an "Herb Affair" was held at a local park. I invited my daughter and her friend to join me at this event. There we heard an inspiring talk on herbs by Pat Welsh, who was introduced as "the Julia Child of gardening" and the author of Southern California Gardening (1992). In addition to writing for Sunset Magazine for years and producing videos for Home and Garden Magazine, she has some shows on the Home and Garden TV channel.

Pat explained that her parents weren't raised to be parents; no fault of their own, they just weren't raised that way. They were rich and suffered the "big crash" during the Depression. "Mother divorced Dad, as she couldn't handle being married to someone who didn't make money," she explained in her matter-of-fact way.

Pat said she and her siblings were left in England, when she was seven, for a whole year. Her mother had to leave and went to America during the war. That childhood set the stage for her emotional connection with plants.

The title of this article came from a phrase she said with glee: "Nature adopted me." Even in such turbulence, she remembers a happy childhood. Not able to connect emotionally to either of her parents or her nurse, and, being English, she couldn't complain about anything. She found solace and happiness in her environment.

When she came to America to be with her mother, she found herself in Hollywood, with manicured lawns and studio sets. She felt no connection to them. One day when she went up into the hills and walked among the sagebrush, she was flooded with childhood memories from the smells she encountered. So far away from her childhood home in England, she had found her place again. Pat tells about her emotional connection to nature in her second book: All My Edens (1996).

As she spoke, her love and ease around plants showed her deep passion. One minute she hugged and stroked a rosemary plant, and the next minute she picked up a knife and hacked off half of the root ball. She then found a longer root and wrapped it around the base of the plant to strangle it and set it in a dish for a bonsai arrangement.

However, life again dealt her a couple of painful blows. Her spirit seems undaunted, nevertheless.

continued on page 180

179

continued from page 179

First, her husband died. She found solace for her grief in her gardens and work with plants. They provide her with emotional nourishment, and she trusts that would continue to be there, as they had been in existence for centuries.

Her second blow came when she developed a bad knee. She had to have a "helper" assist her in her work as she suffered continued problems from a failed knee-replacement operation. She demonstrated her remarkable forgiveness again when she said, "Doctors make mistakes, which happens; so you just get on with your life."

The spirit of this woman and the home she finds in her "nature family" is a reminder to us all to use and find the source of our own resilience. Coming from troubled families or troubled times, and being delivered life blows, does not mean that cannot be overcome. Life's blows do not always rob us of all the joys of our childhood, nor of the pleasures and meaning in our lives. Like Pat, life must be dealt with; there is little escape from adversity. Blows that seem unbearable are especially challenging. Our hope, though, can sometimes be found in our individual passions, which may be blinded from us in our most turbulent times.

* * *

Finding ways to heal your traumatic blows is a long-term process. Your journey may not lead you to a discovery of being adopted by nature. However, I hope this story about Pat Walsh suggests some ideas for your own coping strategies.

Please let me hear from you about the ways that you have found to cope so I can pass them on to others to help them in finding their own personal resiliencies.

Make the Most of Today

Anonymous

Imagine there is a bank that credits your account each morning with $86,400. It carries over no balance from day to day. Every evening deletes whatever part of the balance you failed to use during the day. What would you do? Draw out every cent, of course!

You have such a bank. Its name is Time. Every morning, it credits you with 86,400 seconds. Every night it writes off, as lost, whatever of this you have failed to invest to good purpose.

It carries over no balance. It allows no overdraft. Each day it opens a new account for you. If you fail to use the day's deposit, the loss is yours. There is no going back. There is no drawing against the "tomorrow."

You must live in the present on today's deposits. Invest it so as to get from it the utmost in health, happiness, and success! Make the most of today:

- To realize the value of one year, ask a student who failed a grade.

- To realize the value of one month, ask a mother who gave birth to a premature baby.

- To realize the value of one week, ask the editor of a weekly newspaper.

- To realize the value of one day, ask a daily wage laborer with kids to feed.

- To realize the value of one hour, ask the lovers who are waiting to meet.

- To realize the value of one minute, ask a person who missed the train.

- To realize the value of one second, ask a person who just avoided an accident.

- To realize the value of one millisecond, ask the person who won a silver medal in the Olympics.

Dawn V.

September 5, 2001

Dawn: night, aurora, memory—all are words used to describe my name. My name, betrothed to me before birth. It is an unbroken promise between best friends; a name that has lived through death. Like the brilliant golden sun, embracing the sky with a majestic fiery glow, colors so rich they are inescapable from your stare, and as you focus on the massive fireball, the light grows like an enraged forest fire.

It is a name given to me by my mother, in tribute to her best friend. A friend so true, she sacrificed her life to save another's. Valor one could only dream of possessing, like a soldier in battle. A girl like that I would have liked to have met; so free, so innocent, and bursting with dreams, like shining stars.

Although she passed on in 1975 at the mere age of 13, her memory lives on and will never be forgotten so long as I live. My name, a promise a young girl made to her lost best friend ... for saving her life. Tragedy, like the black of night, only to be erased by the onset of an early Dawn.

Clara Rose

In 1979, Wendy Rose was ten years old. She and her brother lived in Los Gatos with their mother, Clara, who was completing a degree in journalism from San Jose State. The children spent weekends with their dad, from whom Clara was separated. One Sunday afternoon when he brought them home, uniformed policemen met them at the door. Their father was arrested, questioned, then released, and the children went home with him. That night, he told them that their mother was dead.

"We never went back to our house," Wendy told the listeners at the Vigil. "We never went back to say good-bye to our friends, never even went back to Los Gatos." Suddenly they had a new life, a new home, a new family, a new school. Wendy was profoundly angry, but no one noticed. She had dreams of revenge, as well as vivid dreams that her mother was still alive, "and I hated to wake up." She felt completely alienated from all the children at her school, whose lives were so different.

One day when the recess bell rang, Wendy suddenly felt as if she were floating above all the other kids on the playground, looking down on them. From that day, she deliberately repressed every memory of her mother and the crime, and didn't speak about either for ten years. She went to school, started a family, and was well on her way in life, until she learned that the police had a suspect in her mother's murder.

In fact they had always had a suspect, someone she knew, although it is very unlikely that he will ever be brought to justice. After Wendy learned the horrible details of the crime and began to think about it again, she began to fall apart. "I thought I was going crazy," she said. She began having nightmares and fits of rage so severe that she had to quit her job. Finally, she knew she needed help and got in touch with Survivors of Violent Loss for counseling and group therapy.

To her relief, she found that everyone in her group had experienced the same feelings. In talking with them and hearing their stories, she realized that the problems she had were universal among homicide survivors and began the slow process of restoring her equilibrium and her mother's memory. "Now I can think about my mother the way she was in life, not obsess over the way she died."

Recently, Wendy visited her maternal uncle for the first time in twenty years and learned things she had never known about her mother. Clara Rose was energetic and active. She made her own clothes in high school and had been extremely excited about buying her first car, a red convertible. "They tell me she was a free spirit," Wendy said with a proud smile.

Wendy can now also remember how much her mother loved her. She edited the PTA newsletter, coached Wendy's soccer team, and encouraged her to study

continued on page 184

continued from page 183

piano, violin, and singing. She was teaching her daughter how to sew at the time she was murdered, all the time attending school as a single parent.

After what she has gone through, Wendy knows that immediate counseling for children in such situations is crucial, and has studied psychology, planning to become a therapist and work with children who have suffered severe trauma. "If I hadn't repressed things so deeply, I might have named my daughter after my mother."

The following is my dedication to Mom:

> *The wretched tears of grief*
> *I will come to know*
> *as the fiend builds with us his home*
> *through his obscurity*
> *we can't see*
> *that he hides within a healers coat*
> *the serpent that is he*
> *from a crown of bloody slivers*
> *his putrid soul was framed*
> *the slivers pierce and gouge his skin*
> *still, he hides well*
> *the secret from within*
> *but soon*
> *my wretched tears of grief*
> *will turn to acid*
> *on his open skin*
> *and all who worship him will know*
> *for whom he is a kin*
> *not a healer at all*
> *but satins heinous angel*
> *of callous death is him*
>
> > For my mother who was murdered
> > in 1979 when I was only 10

As reported in Victims Voice of Survivors Speech, Wendy Rose at the Victim Assistance Coordinating Council Candlelight Vigil.

Chuck's Story

Unsolved!

Heather, age 16

My journey with heartache began March 1st, 1998. I was pulling weeds in the front yard when I got a call from Heather's mother. Her voice was stressed and she asked me to sit down. That was when I knew Heather was dead. My life was not prepared for what was to follow. Heather's body was discovered dumped on a remote rural highway in Kansas. She had been dead three or four days. Cause of death was blunt-force trauma to the head and strangulation. She was sixteen years old. Heather was like a daughter to me.

Heather was gifted in the subject of literature. She loved to read and write stories, poetry, or songs. She loved to sing. You could name a Disney film and she could sing the musical score from memory. Heather was fun to be with and she was also difficult. She was stubborn and had trouble with any kind of authority. You could say she was a troubled soul. She would rather be homeless, living on the road with strangers, than be in any structured environment. She was known to hitchhike with truckers, or anyone, for that matter. I've always felt Heather was trying to outrun her own personal emotional pain.

There is not a day that goes by that I wish I had Heather and the headaches that went along with her, than to be dealing with pain and heartache for the rest of my life.

Survivors of Violent Loss Program

www.svlp.org

Re-Member-ing Loved Ones with Momentos

This beautiful cabinet was donated by Chuck in memory of Heather to the Survivors of Violent Loss Program to hold precious mementos of lost loved ones.

I Wish Angelina Could Have Known Her Daddy

by Ana

It is still very hard for Ana to talk about what happened in October 2000, when Larry was stabbed to death by his brother-in-law. With her two-year-old daughter in her arms and with a friend at her side for support, Ana recounted through her tears how the murderer laughed about killing Larry.

Ana and Larry had been happily planning for their baby's birth. Like any pair of expectant parents, they had many hopes and dreams for their first child's future and for themselves. Larry worked as a plumber while Ana was pursuing a degree in criminal justice. But in one horrible moment, all their dreams of a long life together were destroyed.

"If I could only have three wishes, this is what they would be," she told the listeners at the Vigil. "I wish the killer had gotten life in prison instead of the seven-year sentence he did receive. I would have loved for my daughter to have the chance to know her daddy. And I wish I could have had the chance to say good-bye."

Walk in My Shoes . . .

Comments from survivors of violent loss:

No one understands this; it leaves you with a body with no life in it.

Said by a sister of a brother who was a murder victim
and lost her last remaining family member in 1998

———————

I miss everything about my son! I am proud to have been his mother! He wasn't perfect, but he was my first-born, my baby, my adult son, my flesh and blood. I miss his smile, his voice, his **"I love you mom,"** *his daily phone call, his laugh, and the feel of his hug.*

I am a Christian and know he is with God; however, I am sick of hearing "He is in a better place than we are." I am sick of hearing "You will see him someday." I am sick of hearing "God needed him more than you did." **Someone even said to me***, "I wonder if God will make you forget him since he is in hell as suicide is a sin." I wanted to lash out, but instead I said that my God loves his children! He gave his own son to die on the cross for our sins! God does not hold an illness against them. I know people mean well, but they should think before they speak. Why not just say something like "MY PRAYERS ARE WITH YOU AT THIS HORRIBLE TIME OF GRIEF." Hold my hand and let me speak of him.* **I need to speak of him.**

GOD BLESS!"

Rosemarie

———————

"Think of it this way: You were going to be pushing him out of the house in the next few years anyway. You just happened to get his room back a little early."

Said to parents whose son took his own life

———————

After a conversation about "triggers" and how they can arise under the most innocuous of circumstances":

Yesterday afternoon I was at Fashion Valley finishing up my Xmas shopping. I popped into the Discovery Channel Store to see if there was anything of interest. As my gaze ranged over some big, juicy, coffee-table books, one caught my eye: "Crime Scene." The "coroner's stamp" font they used was made to be sensational. A few years ago, I would have immediately thought of my dad's crime scene—right in the middle of an otherwise pleasurable expedition.

Turning away from that, I continued to look, focusing on the store's always interesting selection of videos. There were at least four or five "Forensic Files" and "Cold Case Files" videos, with disturbing imagery on the packaging, which was clearly meant to titillate, and sell.

Phew! The land mines are all over; just an observation.

Marina, 2003

(The case against the alleged killer ended in a mistrial and the defendant was not retried.)

Get a Grip!

A sister asks in a case that doesn't turn out favorably, why the killer gets involuntary manslaughter when her brother was shot in the back five times?

DA says: "Get a Grip! It's not the end of the world."

Her reply: **"It was for my brother!"**

The following comments were sent after an email inquiry of how Survivors were being impacted by 9/11 . . .

My grief has resurfaced with vengeance since 9/11. My thoughts of my son, stepson, and mother are almost constant. I really did not tie it into 9/11 until I got your email. But upon reflecting, I realize that since 9/11 my thoughts have been filled with sadness over my losses. Sometimes the grief is absolutely overwhelming. I have been in mourning again. I do not feel right wearing colors. I find myself yearning more and more for the comfort of prayer, and at the same time find it more difficult to pray. The future is uncertain and that causes a certain amount of fear and apprehension. I wish I could say that I have been nicer to people, but I actually have closed people out. I find myself keeping people at a distance. I was even told a couple of weeks ago that I am mean. I am not trying to be, but in an effort to protect myself I do keep people at a distance. Especially my family, which is very painful.

Anonymous

_____

9/11 has brought fear and uncertainty. It has brought to the forefront feelings of grief I thought I had worked through. I feel very isolated and yet do not necessarily want to end that isolation. It somehow feels safer. Anyway, those are my thoughts. How do they compare with others? Am I completely off my rocker? Take care. Lots of love,

Patti

_____

We are all just doing our best. Denial helps. If we were acutely aware of every danger in our lives we would be paralyzed. Look at all the centuries of strife in the world. We are only babies. We will do fine adjusting and surviving. Especially with all of the love and hope we have. Love you,

Anonymous

_____

Honestly, I do not think I have reacted any differently to 9/11 than I would if I had not previously suffered a violent loss. I was devastated, I grieved, and since I have tried to be that much more supportive of our troops and family members who are working to protect our nation. PTSD did not kick in as it did with the Van Dam Case. I hope this was helpful.

Kelly R.

_____

I was traumatized all over again by this event. I actually thought in a weird way that "America" knows how we as survivors of violent death feel now. At least for a moment. . . . I certainly would not wish this event on anyone. I hope that fate guides me to JUSTICE & TRUTH. God Bless America . . .

Cherry M.

———————

The Thought that I have is the greatest sadness for the victims' families and how their loved ones' lives were robbed from them. I have invasive thoughts that there are people out there who are actively waiting, stalking, and planning to harm the people of our nation at any moment on such a great magnitude and in such a violent manner. That affects our waking moments so often; it impedes many activities and contributes to the breakdown of our mental wellness—even as a nation. Our determination as a people and a nation not to lose any more is comforting. I pray we are successful.

Dee

———————

I feel that being close to family is more important than it has even been since 9/11. It has also made me worry about what could happen next. I'm nervous about foreigners and worry what they will do next.

Nina R.

"I Know How You Feel"

While sitting in the lounge waiting for my car to be serviced, I started chatting with a teacher who said she worked with immigrants from Africa. She said she was touched by the lives they lived before coming to our country. She felt deeply their struggles of living here and living with past events that drove them to find refuge in another world. She mentioned many had witnessed the murder of their loved ones. I told her about our work in building a resource nationally for Survivors of Violent Loss.

She then asked with great sincerity: *Why is it so bad to say to someone: I know how you feel?*

Of course, I answered her and then sent an email query to some survivors to give them an opportunity to reply.

Here are some of their remarks: (to read all of the replies, click on the Support tab on our Web page at: www.svlp.org.)

> *The attempt to empathize is futile. There simply is no way you Really Can Know. You have no basis for this emotion until it has been felt through a loss of your own. To say "you know how I feel" makes it seem like an attempt to minimize the pain I am feeling, which is impossible. There is no bottom to the depth of the pain I feel. The words make my heart hurt a little more. Just let it be. It cannot be blanketed so easily. It is best just to sympathize, best to regret that this has happened. Best to simply hold me and let me weep.*
>
>

Dee
Aunt of Tara, age 20,
murdered 12/21/84

> *To those who say, "I know just how you feel"—I pray to all the Gods there are that you DON'T know just how I feel.*
>
> *This statement is often followed by another statement, "My (sister/husband/ whatever) died a few (weeks/months) ago." And if I inquire further, it was usually a slower death, of some illness or other, and by the time the person finally died, it was a blessing to all concerned. There was no surprise. If someone dies an expected death, the estate is settled before the death, the heirlooms are pre-dealt with. There's a good start on the mourning. A natural death is nice and clean, and is part of the natural order.*
>
> *The trouble with sudden death, especially murder, is that it isn't nice and clean—no matter how good and organized your life was before that, hold on. Suddenly, the cops are questioning your neighbors about your possible collusion in the death; there's worry about trouble-maker strangers (media and otherwise) showing up at the funeral; there's being dragged through years of trials (or worse, never seeing justice trying to get done); there's being hounded by the press; there's a bumper crop of shock, anger, guilt, loss, pressure, and confusion, not to mention full-blown depression.*

You find mourning particularly hard. You find that you have to be polite to defense attorneys (a particularly low form of life), and your best friends get it with both barrels sometimes. It isn't natural, and it goes on and on.

People whose loved ones are murdered, killed in car wrecks, fires, etc.—we're blazing our own trails through the human psyche and writing our own books. Sudden death isn't new, but it's never been openly discussed from our point of view. We hardly know from one day to the next how we feel.

Don't tell me that you know "just how I feel," just because your Mother was lucky enough to die at her third heart attack. For starts, you don't know how much I envy you . . .

Bonnie

––––––––––––

Thanks for your request for our comments. I really believe people "mean well" when they say they know how we feel, but they really can't know unless they have experienced a traumatic loss. We know of someone who said this and commented the reason they knew how the loss felt was because they had lost a pet dog! I think people who want to help do best when they just sit quietly with us as we cry and/or talk about our loved one. Words are not necessary or comforting—just the presence of one who "feels" with us, who allows us to express the pain, the sorrow, the anger without judging us.

Our son was murdered in 1990, and his body has not been found, and we did not know for almost nine years what happened to him. We "knew" something terrible had happened to him, but until one of the two killers confessed, we were living a paradox—hoping Tim might be alive somewhere and at the same time trying to accept the reality that he was dead.

P.P.M.

––––––––––––

Dear Connie,

I continue to be amazed by the replies of people and question what motivates them to want to ask a question like that. So many beliefs are changing for me, sometimes daily. I wonder if anyone can really know "How" a person feels when in the midst of loss, even for those who have experienced a similar event. Perhaps that is the clue, similar. Yet when you come down to it—one just can NEVER KNOW. I believe that is a very personal relationship belonging to the person experiencing it and needs to be honored, held, comforted, and cared for like a newborn with love. Without being intrusive or demanding of it to be anything other than what it is—beginning and growing, tender and vulnerable.

Larry

The Homicide Diet

When you've tried everything, and nothing has worked, this diet is 95% guaranteed. However, there is no money-back guarantee because the diet is totally FREE to any unsuspecting co-victim! Any family member may start this diet at any time. The ideal time would be just before bathing suit season (March is a good month, as the photos of rail-thin models in bikinis are just beginning to grace the pages of fashion magazines.)

If you follow the diet religiously (if you still have any religion to believe in) by June, you can lose a good 20+ pounds. Keep in mind that results may vary from person to person due to grieving and mourning differences. It must be stressed that this is a no fad diet. Given the number of people killed every day, it looks like this diet is here to stay!

Actually, the Homicide Diet has been around for a while (longer than we like to think), but has never been recognized as an official weight-loss program. Along with all the other needed changes and additions to various laws, with your help, maybe this diet can become official in the near future. Here are some suggested guidelines (and remember everyone is different, so don't feel that you must follow them exactly or that the sequence will be the same for everyone):

1. When taking anti-depressants, sleeping pills and tranquilizers in order to survive each day, your appetite—if you even have one—will probably be non-existent. Although, it isn't necessary to take drugs to lose your desire to eat. It just happens naturally (lucky you!). You will also have no energy to eat, as it will take everything you have inside just to make it from moment to moment.

2. If you do happen to have even a fleeting feeling of hunger, it probably won't last. This is good, as any food put in front of you will most likely make you want to vomit. Of course, if you do actually vomit, this is even better, as then there are no added calories to worry about.

3. If you do manage to eat a few bites, don't worry that you've gone off your diet and punish yourself needlessly. You've been punished enough. Those three or four bites will last at least a week. This also helps by taking the difficulty out of determining correct portion size. (No weighing of food on that ridiculous scale is involved.)

4. Not to worry, because by the time you decide to eat again (don't fret about how much time has gone by, because you won't be able to figure it out, and you certainly don't need one more thing to agonize over!) steps two and three will happen all over again.

5. This diet is so easy, due to the fact that you may be in a rather zombie-like state for quite a while, reliving the above steps repeatedly. But, don't panic; this non-functional, almost-catatonic-state is quite normal, even though you think you've lost your mind. Just remember . . . it's not your mind you've lost, just your child, father, mother, sister, brother, wife, husband, aunt, uncle, or whomever it was that was murdered. But, of course, you can console yourself with the fact that, yes, you've lost a beloved family member, but you are also losing weight! And, after all, isn't that the goal?

6. This diet is much easier than following a protein diet, a carbohydrate diet, a sugar-busters diet, etc., as some days—if you have the strength to open the box and you can remember where it is—you may only eat 3 or 4 malted milk balls for breakfast, lunch, and dinner. (Refer to steps 2 and 3 again.) The diet requires no mixing of anything (which is good, since you have no energy or desire to turn on the Cuisinart) or looking at charts to figure out the difference between a protein and a carbohydrate.

7. Stomach aches and constipation may present problems, but again, don't panic; every part of your body has shut down, so why not your stomach and intestines, too! It just adds to your lack of desire to eat, which is a basic theory of this diet. This can be a problem, however, as a bloated belly tends to make you look like you've gained weight, when you really haven't. Keep in mind that you're right on track, and don't give up. (This advice also pertains to when you feel like you don't want to live another moment and are seriously considering killing yourself.) I promise you that the weight will fall off!

8. As your diet progresses, your wardrobe can be either a problem or not, depending on how you look at it. Remember . . . attitude is everything! When people look at you and ask if your belt is too big— "My God! It could go around you twice!"—it may be quite flattering and reassuring to know you are meeting your objectives. Or, you face the possibility of declaring bankruptcy because you've spent so much money on a new wardrobe because nothing fits. This also could cause overcrowded closets. You may have to make a decision (hopefully not) as to whether or not to give away your old clothes. Of course, this is hard to do, as you never know if you'll ever be back to your pre-homicide weight and should save them. And, debtor's prison could be quite attractive. What else could possibly happen to you any more horrible? Additionally, if your murdered loved-one's clothes, shoes and other doo-dads have been sent back to you, there is always the dilemma as to where to store them. If you're like me, you've made room in a closet in the spare

bedroom for all those things. This further complicates the situation. But again, by moving everything around constantly, you may even lose more weight. You're that much closer to your goal! See what I mean about attitude?!

9. When, and if, you manage to go out to dinner with friends after awhile, there may be considerable guilt on their part. This happens because you are sitting with a salad in front of you, only eating a few bites, if that. They have just finished a four-course dinner. They feel guilty (and maybe a little envious) because you're not eating, and they have just pigged-out. They are trying to cheer you up, which is a fruitless effort. They may also feel very fat and concerned that they have gone off their diet, which is, of course, totally inferior to yours. The way around this issue is to remind them why you started dieting in the first place. Hopefully, that will work and not cause more guilt on their part! But, then again, that rather disturbing revelation may contribute further to their guilt, and they really won't know what to do or say.

10. Again, remember that results may vary from person to person. Some mourners may actually gain weight. As the shock of trying desperately to cope with the murder of a loved one begins to wear off and the reality starts to set in, food may be the only thing that provides an inkling of comfort. Of course, if this happens, go for it! Moments (or seconds) of comfort (if you are lucky enough to have any) are usually not maintained for very long.

Cory's Devastated Mom

Appendix IV

Heroes, Finding Meaning and Making a Difference

Song for Brad by Stephanie Rogers
Hope Gallery
An Extraordinary Life: Robert Del Conte
Paradoxical Commandments by Kent M. Keith
He Gave His Life to Save Three Others
In Memory of Dianne (9/11)
Candy Lightner: Founder of MADD
Finding Peace in Photographs: Beverly Myers Bailey
Dia de los Muertos (Day of the Dead)
Suicide Memorial Wall
Yvonne Pointer
Cathy and Janelle's College Reunion
Jonathan Sellers and Charlie Keever Outdoor Educational
    Activity Center
Memorial Honoring 53
Cathryne Anne Mueller Memorial Plaque
Sam's Bench

See more examples in Appendix III.

Song for Brad

By Stephanie Rogers

 Written for survivor writer Austin's nephew.

36 years
can't count the tears
which fall before
your life of labor

the youngest child
so brave and mild
a family
of grace and beauty

you couldn't turn your heart away
from feeling someone else's pain
a heart so strong
a life not long enough

you gave your life
for others' rights
and now you've won
a silent freedom

you couldn't turn your eyes away
from hardships others have to face
a heart so strong
a life not long enough

you heard a call
to rise and follow
the road unpaved,
forgotten way,
a sign of grace

you couldn't turn your head away
from all the troubles others face
a heart so strong
a life not long enough

you lived so much
for truth you sought
left not in vain
but to make change

you'd never turn yourself away
from helping someone else feel safe
a heart so strong
a life not long enough, not long enough ...

you may be gone
never forgotten

An Extraordinary Life—Robert Del Conte

Robert Del Conte founded the San Felipe Humanitarian Association and headed a group home for foster children on a ranch in New Mexico. He was among the first Americans allowed into war-torn Kosovo to oversee humanitarian relief efforts.

While driving home one evening in October 2001, Mr. Del Conte stopped to help a man whose car appeared to be disabled. The man stole his wallet, knocked him out and slit his throat, then threw him into a gully, where his body was found three days later. The murderer was apprehended when he used Mr. Del Conte's credit card at a local tourist stop.

"We worried about him when he was overseas in a war zone—we never thought he'd be murdered in his own home town," said his daughter, Belissa Davis. Ms. Davis and her five siblings grew up on the ranch in New Mexico. "He murdered my father for the price of a steak-and-eggs breakfast at Denny's and one night at a hotel," she continued. "My father lost his life for sixty dollars."

Enduring the pain

After the initial shock and horror, the Del Conte family found themselves at the center of a painful investigative process that put them all "under a microscope." The media "dragged my father's name through the mud," questioning Mr. and Mrs. Del Conte's entire way of life, and speculating that their work with problem children had put them at risk.

Even after the trial, at which the perpetrator, subject to the "three-strikes law," was sentenced to 22 years, Ms. Davis found that the simplest task brought tears to her eyes. "I just had to have faith that the next day wouldn't be as bad as this one."

"You've got to get through the firsts, seconds, and the lasts," Ms. Davis told the assembled crowd of more than 120 people, many of whom had lost loved ones to violence. "My father never saw his first granddaughter, and he didn't get to attend my wedding."

An inspirational message she found when cleaning out her father's desk vividly illustrated his strength and commitment. "The good you do today, people will often forget tomorrow. Do good anyway."

This was displayed on Robert Del Conte's desk and contributed by Ms. Davis. (As printed in the *Victims Voice*, Vol. 14, Number 4, June 2002.)

(See the entire sentiment in Kent Keith's *Paradoxical Commandments* on the next page.)

Paradoxical Commandments

1. People are illogical, unreasonable, and self-centered. Love them anyway.

2. If you do good, people will accuse you of selfish ulterior motives. Do good anyway.

3. If you are successful, you will win false friends and true enemies. Succeed anyway.

4. The good you do today will be forgotten tomorrow. Do good anyway.

5. Honesty and frankness make you vulnerable. Be honest and frank anyway.

6. The biggest men and women with the biggest ideas can be shot down by the smallest men and women with the smallest minds. Think big anyway.

7. People favor underdogs but follow only top dogs. Fight for a few underdogs anyway.

8. What you spend years building may be destroyed overnight. Build anyway.

9. People really need help but may attack you if you do help them. Help people anyway.

10. Give the world the best you have and you'll get kicked in the teeth. Give the world the best you have anyway.

The Paradoxical Commandments were written by Kent M. Keith as part of his book, *The Silent Revolution: Dynamic Leadership in the Student Council*, published in 1968 by Harvard Student Agencies, Cambridge, Massachusetts.

www.paradoxicalcommandments.com

He Gave His Life to Save Three Others

Vincent Paul Thomas, age 40, lived from 1961-2001. He was an EMT, firefighter, private pilot, and an entrepreneur with his own Rocky Mountain Red-Dirt T-Shirt line. He ran a country store, and a girl that worked with him was being abused by her live-in boyfriend. Being a single mother with two small children, the girl asked for refuge at her boss's house. Her boyfriend came over with a gun to get her and the kids. Vince blocked the way and ended up being shot three times. He gave his life to save three others—as was his way.

In loving memory,

Mom

In Memory of Dianne

Marine Guests Help Ease 9/11 Sadness

A story By Elena Gaona, staff writer of *The San Diego Union-Tribune*, on November 26, 2004, describes the following:

> There is still that vision, ingrained in her sister's head, of a young Dianne Gladstone with a huge turkey leg in her hand. "She'd take big bites out of it. It covered her whole face," said Jayne Marx yesterday as she prepared a Thanksgiving meal in honor of her late sister.
>
> Dianne Gladstone, 55, was one of the 2,626 people who died in New York's World Trade Center on Sept. 11, 2001.
>
> The Marx family honors Gladstone and gave thanks for a "blessed life" by inviting young Marines from Camp Pendleton to share the holiday with them.
>
> "I'm thankful we have such a blessed life," Marx said. "I feel strongly these Marines are risking their lives for us so we can have that life."

Candy Lightner: Founder of
Mothers Against Drunk Driving (MADD)

David J. Hanson, PhD, tells us on the MADD website about its founder, Candy Lightner. In 1980, Candy's 13-year-old daughter Cari was killed by a drunk, hit-and-run driver as she walked down a street. Candy vowed to fight against this needless homicide.

The drunken drive had been found guilty and convicted four times of drunk driving. The fifth time, he killed Cari and received a two-year prison sentence. He spent time serving his sentence in a work camp and halfway house and avoided prison.

The sentence leniency outraged Ms. Lightner who then organized Mothers Against Drunk Drivers (MADD), later changed to Mothers Against Drunk Driving. Her mission was to raise public awareness of the serious nature of drunken driving and to promote tough legislation against the crime.

Before this crusade, drunken driving was not taken seriously. Comedians were known for getting laughs for impersonating drunken people. Intoxication was accepted as an excuse for such behavior.

Candy Lightner appeared on major television shows, spoke before the US Congress, addressed professional and business groups, and worked tirelessly for years to change public attitudes, modify judicial behavior and promote tough new legislation.

In 1983, President Ronald Reagan bestowed upon her the President's Volunteer Action Award, and she was the subject of the movie "Mothers Against Drunk Drivers: The Candy Lightner Story."

Finding Peace in Photographs: Beverly Myers Bailey

"I founded Healing Imagery in 2001, after my brother was murdered, and I found that photographing beautiful images has helped me heal," Ms. Bailey said. "Living just outside the New York area at the time of 9/11, I discovered I was not alone in my desire to be surrounded by soothing and peaceful artwork."

A percentage of all Ms. Bailey's sales goes to support victim advocacy groups.

She said, "I believe in the power of photography to promote healing and to inspire feelings of hope and peace in the hearts of those who have suffered. I have my photography hanging in New York City in the Action Against Hunger office, which deals with starving children throughout the world."

Her works also hang in medical offices, cancer clinics, and wellness centers, and she is "most proud of the photography I have hanging in the Washington, DC, Superior Courthouse waiting area for witnesses and family members of violent crime."

Ms. Bailey recently exhibited her work at the Providence Biltmore Hotel for the 20th Anniversary Gala of The Blackstone Valley Advocacy Center, a program working to end domestic violence. She said she hopes to continue doing shows that benefit such charities and is interested in connection with advocacy groups on the Cape and in Massachusetts.

"If my photography can bring a moment's peace to anyone that has suffered, I am gratified," she said.

Ms. Bailey's website is www.healingimagery.com.

Dia de los Muertos

Survivors of Violent Loss honors loved ones who participate in a the traditional Mexican observation of "Dia de los Muertos" (Day of the Dead). This cultural event, which is also observed throughout the southwestern US, focuses on gatherings of family and friends to remember those who have died. Traditions include building private altars—called *ofrendas*—and honoring the deceased by leaving sugar skulls, marigolds, and favorite foods and possessions of their loved ones at the altars.

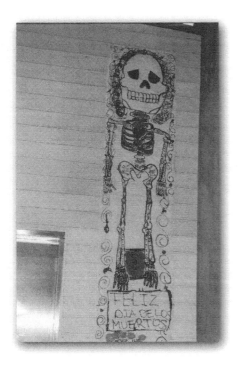

Suicide Memorial Wall

The Suicide Memorial Wall was created on 15 April 2001 to help us remember some of the names of people from all over the world whose deaths were self-inflicted.

www.suicidememorialwall.com

Yvonne Pointer

www.yvonnepointer.com/

On December 6, 1984, Yvonne's 14-year-old daughter, Gloria, was abducted, raped and brutally murdered. Her murder remains unsolved. The ways she has emerged from the ashes of this event include the establishment of the Gloria Pointer Scholarship Fund to assist underprivileged students with college, and she has authored two books: Behind the Death of a Child and Word from the Mother.

Cathy and Janelle's College Reunion

This is a "nostalgic and haunting story of a life interrupted, but then continued in a parallel universe." Earth Day—April 22, 2015—will be the 35th anniversary of my daughter Sheryl's murder. As fellow survivors, you may wonder why I've written this short piece of semi-biographical fiction about a girl long gone.

With all my best wishes,

Ellen Zelda Kessner

http://www.amazon.com/Cathy-Janelles-College-Reunion-Kessner-ebook/dp/B00HFGMNWA

The Jonathan Sellers & Charlie Keever Foundation

The foundation was formed by Dennis Sellers and Milena (Sellers) Phillips in 2005. Its mission is to promote the safety and well-being of children through education and to support families who have lost loved ones at the hands of another.

On March 27, 1993, two best friends, 9-year-old Jonathan and 13-year-old Charlie, left home for a bike ride on a beautiful March morning and never returned. Their ride was cut short when a sexual predator murdered them both. For eight years their case went unsolved. In 2001, the murderer was finally found through a DNA database. In April 2004, a jury voted unanimously for the death penalty. On September 1, 2004, a California judge sentenced the murderer to death row at San Quentin State Prison.

The latest project of this busy foundation is the book *Always Fly Away* by Milena (Sellers) Phillips and Deborah Dorn.

Always Fly Away is a children's book written in rhyming verse and tells the story from the perspective of a young bird named Stella. Stella leaves home to meet a friend by the creek, and there she is greeted by a kind-looking cat. The cat seems gentle and asks for Stella's help, but Stella remembers the advice her mother gives her every time she goes out, "Stella remember, Keep your distance from strangers, stay alert, and when you don't know what to do, Away Fly Away." This saves her life when the cat shows his true intentions as he tries to grab her, claws extended. With this story Milena is able to bring Stella home safely—a wish she has for every child.

To learn more about this foundation, go to: www.jsck.org.

To buy the book, go to: www.reflectivepublishing.com.

Little Rock Air Force Base Memorial

Jacksonville Air Force Base, Jacksonville, Arkansas

Memorial Honoring 53

Not all Soldiers wear uniforms and carry rifles. Those civilian workers who went into the Titan II Missile Complex near Searcy, August 9, 1965, were dressed in work clothes, wore hard hats, carried hammers and paint brushes, but who's to say they were not soldiers? The 53 workers who were trapped when an explosion piped through the missile silo gave up the greatest gift any soldier anywhere could give—his life. Their sacrifice and that of their families is no less than any other. We gratefully acknowledge these men and dedicate this monument to their memory with love and respect.

We Miss You.

In Memory of Sam Knott

Founder of Crime Victims Oak Garden, from your poker buddies.

Cathryne Anne Mueller

Cathryne Anne Mueller is honored by friends and family so that she will not be forgotten.

She lived her life giving to those less fortunate. A plaque honoring her is in a permanent place in a building in Hollywood that serves those who are less fortunate.

"She gave her time and love to the homeless and needy. Her spirit will always remain among us."

November 30, 1970—August 7, 1997

POMC (Parents of Murdered Children), Maine Chapter

The group established a memorial in 2014 to remember murdered loved ones and have a dedication of new names added annually.

Appendix V

Support Groups

Forming a "Journey" Support Group
Support Group Guidelines
Restorative Retelling Interventions
Resources on Resiliency

Forming a "Journey" Support Group

by Connie Saindon, MFT

1. **Two Facilitators:** Work with two of you to start this group; co-facilitators work best. Check your schedules to make sure you can keep the time commitment and you have nothing that will interfere. This is a closed, time-limited group process, and we ask folks who sign up to attend each meeting, the same that we ask of you. Clear your schedule to make sure it is free to do the group. Let friends and family know of your commitment to gain their support as well.

2. **Location:** Obtain a location that you can have for three hours, once a week, for at least ten weeks.

3. **Spread the word** to your community agencies and contacts. Use group email and ask folks to spread the word. Hand out a flyer that has time, location, and contact information for anyone who has questions or may want to participate.

4. **Not for everyone.** This group is designed to help folks learn ways to manage the intense emotions that are normal for a violent loss. **It can be too soon** for someone, even if it is many years since the death.

5. **Do a Pre-participation Interview.** During interviews you may notice an individual's inability to be able to listen as well as talk to you. It is best that the interview not take place in a public area; i.e., coffee house or restaurant. Interviewees need to be free to express their pain. A public place may prohibit this. Also, individuals may be stuck in anger and seeking justice. If so, they may not be ready for this group. **Their distress may still be too raw** and immediate. They may need individual support/therapy first.

6. **Some disorders are not appropriate for the support group.** Active substance abuse, along with some psychiatric disorders, may rule out a participant. It is best they are referred for substance abuse or mental health evaluation for appropriate services. They may be able to attend when these issues have some stabilization.

7. **It is not automatic that someone will be in the grou**p. It is up to you to decide when to add someone to the group. It is important that you commit to not putting them in a process that will be too much for them. This is how you look out for them. They may want to participate, but there still is too much intensity. You can contact them when the next group is forming. Support them in getting additional support to bolster their resiliency.

8. **If participants are in therapy**, it will be important that they inform their therapists of the support group. We have not seen therapy or the support group interfere with the other. You are not therapists, so fully support what your interviewee wants to do, while sticking with your decision as to whether this is the right time for this person to be in the support group.

9. **Ten participants, two hours.** While pre- and post-group time may be needed for the facilitators, the support group runs for ten weeks, with ten participants, for two hours.

The Journey

Support-Group Guidelines

These guidelines are for a self-help support group run by trained facilitators.

The ten-step process is adapted from the Restorative Retelling Model (an evidence-based clinical approach). While the group is not therapy, it may be therapeutic and supplement existing services you are receiving, so it is important to inform other professionals about your participation.

The purpose of the group is to help you learn to live better with the violent loss they have experienced. In order to do this, we ask you to:

1. Commit to attending all ten meetings.

2. Please be on time. The group begins and ends on time.

3. Keep confidentiality. Everything shared in the group is said in confidence and should not to leave the room.

4. Talk about yourself. Use statements such as: I feel, think, believe, want. Sharing your personal experiences will help you get the most out of this group.

5. Say as much or as little as you wish when it is your turn. There is no judgment or pressure to talk.

6. Avoid interruptions. Note: facilitators may do this to guide the group.

7. Give each speaker your full attention. Listen with an open heart when others share.

8. Avoid advice giving. What worked for you may not work for others.

9. Be respectful and compassionate. The horrific wounds each of you has had requires this time of care. Judgments are not helpful here.

10. Attend all meetings. Contact your group facilitator if you are not able to attend, as group members will be concerned about your welfare.

This type of group guideline session will work with the ten-step structure in *The Journey* workbook by Connie Saindon, MFT.

Restorative Retelling Interventions

by Connie Saindon

Restorative Retelling focuses on interventions that act to counterbalance us, to help stabilize us during the intermittent and overwhelming experience of losing someone in a violent way. These interventions are innate; that is, we are born with these capacities. You may not recognize them at first, but you can look to see how others as well as yourself work with these abilities. Your ability to use them may be less successful at first, which is understandable, but in time, you may call on these methods to help you as you learn to live with what has happened to you. Be patient with yourself and others, but keep your focus on the ways you help yourself using your own abilities, along with these interventions. It is normal for your focus to be pulled in many other directions and intensities. However, do take time out to ask yourself how you helped yourself each day, and how your family and friends did so as well.

The Three P's of Restorative Retelling: Pacification, Partitioning, Perspective

These are descriptions of the resiliencies that help and examples that you may find familiar:

Pacification

Pacification is the ability to quiet oneself, to calm down, to self-soothe. Some examples may be practicing the breathing exercises at the end of each of your steps. The more you listen to the exercises, the more you will have the reminder when you really need to. It will become second nature for you to just take a deep breath and hold it in, then slowly let it go. Have a bottle of bubbles available as a reminder as well.

Lavender is for healing

Other examples include noticing something in your world that is not this loss that grabs your attention for a moment or two—a baby, music by Enya, lavender, yoga or meditation practice, balancing your checkbook, and so on). Review the Step Three Breathing Exercise and "Making Sense," which guides you to focus on each of your senses, one at time, to help you quiet down.

T-shirt art that puts the question outside of ourselves and helps to separate.

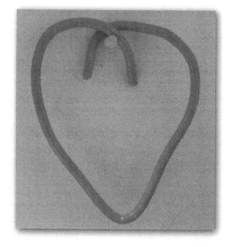

As does this symbol of a loved one who is remembered by a big heart.

As does this symbol remember a brother.

Partitioning

Partitioning is the ability to separate yourself from feeling as if you are one with what has happened, as if you, too, died. In time, as you do activities to describe your loved one in ways that you wish to remember them, you will not be as merged with them as if you had this death happen to you as well. Your ability to represent who they were will be more accurate when you are able to speak of them without this engulfment in the way that they died, which you may experience for some time.

When you describe your loved one's life, such as when we ask you to do so in Step Five, you are using your ability to have them as a separate person. Read some of the examples that the survivor writers use in answering the question: Who was your loved one?

In Step Ten we ask you to select a symbol for your loved one, and that can be represented by something you think was important to them. When you identify them by something important to them, you are using your ability to engage in partitioning. Many of you will say that you felt as if you died, too, but you did not. It is our job to carry the information about who they were to others who come after them. Would your loved ones want to be known by how they died or by how they lived life and what they loved?

You see the symbol for each of those who answered the questions for each step as described in Step Ten. These symbols tell you something about each of the writers' loved ones. Your symbol will do the same. The symbols represent how our loved ones lived, not how they died.

Iris is a symbol of hope.

Perspective

Those who have lost someone in a violent way say that they doubt they will ever feel happiness, joy, or fulfillment in a meaningful way. They anticipate that their lives will be a "going through the motions" kind of life.

The extreme pain of a violent loss may be convincing. Having joy or fun may cause someone to feel disloyal to a loved one. One survivor said she didn't eat for several days because her brother loved to eat.

Our natural ability to have hope for the future has a chance to be regained when we understand the helpful process of **restorative retelli**ng. The Journey helps tell what happened in such a way as to be restorative for the storyteller to counteract being obsessed with how the love one died. Many find they are living a mission or a cause, small or large, in the memory of their loved ones. Examples of such perspectives are in the writings of our survivor writers as well as in Appendix IV.

Resources on Resiliency

Retelling Violent Death, Edward Rynearson (2001). Taylor & Frances Routledge, New York, NY.

In This book, Dr Rynearson presents a strategy for restorative retelling that is based upon his 30 years of clinical practice and research with family members after a violent death.

The Resilient Self: How Survivors of Troubled Families Rise Above Adversity, Steven J. Wolin and Sybil Wolin. Villard, 1993.

The Wolins' chart of different resiliencies is most helpful in that it shows the inner core as what we learn as children and, if all goes well, what we learn as a teen, and what we learn as an adult, which all lead to the core resiliency in the outer ring. The way I understand it is that we have wedges of wounds and wedges of resiliencies. Our resiliencies work to help our wounds. A personal example:

I came from an alcoholic family, so my Relationship wedge can be confusing and difficult for me to figure out, to navigate. However, I liked school. I could focus . . . and excel . . . so my "work" wedge is stronger.

You will find the Wolins' core concepts and more on their website: http://projectresilience.com

Too Scared to Cry: Psychic Trauma in Childhood by Lenore Terr. Basic Books, 1992.

Terr includes excellent examples of what happens to children who are traumatized. The Chowchilla children, who were held underground in a school bus, excelled in school, so reviewers of these children missed many problems that occurred later in their lives. Terr also uses a Stephen King story in her book. The book is easy to read and story-like.

Violent Death: Resilience and Intervention Beyond the Crisis (Routledge Psychosocial Stress Series) Edward K. Rynearson MD. Alison Salloum, Connie Saindon, et al. Routledge, 2006.

Dr. Rynearson's model of Restorative Retelling emphasizes the innate resiliencies we all have: "The loss of a loved one following a violent death is a shocking experience." In this book he has collected views from leaders in the field. Dr Rynearson's work can be found at: http://www.vdbs.org.

Strengthening Family Resilience, edited by Froma Walsh. The Guilford Press, 1998.

Contributors in this book help delineate what families do to shore themselves up in dealing with difficult times.

Group Work with Adolescents After Violent Death, Alison Salloum, PhD. Routledge, 2004. This manual for facilitators of teen grief groups and other mental health professionals addresses the unique needs of adolescents experiencing traumatic reactions in the aftermath of violent death.

Against Terrible Odds: Lessons in Resilience from Our Children, Sol Levine, MD, and Heather Wood Ion. Bull Publishing Co., 2000. The authors show how 12 traumatized children developed into productive, caring, and responsible adults.

Bibliography

Alexander, Caroline (February, 2015). "Behind the Mask: Revealing the Trauma of War." *National Geographic.*

Breslau, N., Davis, G.C., & Andreski, P. (1991). "Traumatic Events and Post-traumatic Stress Disorder in an Urban Population of Young Adults." Archives of *General Psychiatry.* 48, 216-222.

Chappell, Bill (January 14, 2013). *U.S. Military's Suicide Rate Surpassed Combat Deaths in 2012.* National Public Radio. http://www.npr.org/sections/thetwo-way/2013/01/14/169364733/u-s-militarys-suicide-rate-surpassed-combat-deaths-in-2012

Connors, Philip (2015). *All the Wrong Places: A Life Lost and Found.* New York: W. W. Norton & Company. 196.

Cook, J. A. (1983). "A Death in the Family: Parental Bereavement in the First Year." *Suicide and Life Threatening Behavior,* 13(1), 42-61.

Doka, Kenneth, Editor, (1996). *Living with Grief After Sudden Loss: Suicide, Homicide, Accident, Heart Attack, Stroke.* Taylor & Francis, Bristol, PA.

Edwards, Larry M. (2013). *Dare I Call It Murder?: A Memoir of Violent Loss.* Wigeon Publishing, San Diego, CA.

Frankl, V., (1978). *The Unheard Cry for Meaning.* New York: Simon and Schuster.

Figley, Charles, McCubbin, Hamilton, (1983). *Stress and the Family: Coping with Catastrophe.* Bruner Mazel Publishers, New York, NY.

Higgins, Gina O'Connell (1994). *Resilient Adults.* Jossey-Bass Publisher, San Francisco, CA.

Janoff-Bulman, R. (1992). *Shattered Assumptions: Towards a New Psychology of Trauma.* New York: The Free Press.

Jenkins, Bill (2001). *What to Do When the Police Leave: A Guide to the First Days of Traumatic Aftermath.* WJB Press, Richmond, VA.

Klass, Dennis, PhD (1983). *Reflections About Time and Change,* Webster University, St. Louis, MO.

Kulka, R.A., Schlenger, W., & Fairbank, J. (1990). *Trauma and the Vietnam War Generation.* New York: Brunner/Mazel.

Lehman, D. R., Lang, R.L., Wortman, C. B., & Sorenson, S. B. (1987). "Long-term Effects of Losing a Spouse or Child in a Motor Vehicle Crash." *Journal of Personality and Social Psychology,* 52, 218-231.

Levin, Saul, Heather Wood Ion (2002). *Against Terrible Odds, Lessons in Resilience from our Children.* Bull Publishing Company, Boulder, CO.

Lord, Janice (2007). *No Time for Goodbyes, 6th Edition: Coping with Sorrow, Anger and Injustice after a Tragic Death.* Compassion Books, Burnsville, NC.

Murphy, S. A.; Braun, T, Tillery, L., Cain, K.C.; Johnson, C. L., Beaton, R.D. (1999). "PTSD Among Bereaved Parents Following the Violent Deaths of Their 12-28-year-old Children: a longitudinal Prospective Analysis." *Journal of Traumatic Stress Studies,* Vol. 12, No. 2.

Neimeyer, Robert A. (2000). *Constructions of Disorder: Meaning-Making Frameworks for Psychotherapy.* American Psychological Association.

O'Hara, Kathleen. (2006). *A Grief Like No Other: Surviving the Violent Death of Someone You Love,* Marlowe & Company, New York, NY.

Prigerson, H.G., et al. (1995). Traumatic Grief as a Risk Factor for Mental and Physical morbidity. *The American Journal of Psychiatry.* 154:5, 616-623.

Prigerson, H.G., et. al. (1997). "Results of a Consensus Conference to Refine Diagnostic Criteria for Traumatic Grief." *American Journal of Psychiatry.*

Rynearson, E. (2001). *Retelling Violent Death.* Taylor & Frances Routledge, New York, NY.

Rynearson, E., Salloum, Saindon, Sears, Bonnano, Rafael, et al. (2006). *Violent Death, Resilience and Intervention Beyond the Crisis.* Taylor and Frances, New York, NY.

Rynearson, E. (1994). "Psychotherapy of Bereavement After Homicide." *Journal of Psychotherapy Practice and Research,* Vol. 3 (4) 341-347.

Saindon, Connie (2014). *Murder Survivor's Handbook: Real-Life Stories, Tips & Resources.* Wigeon Publishing, San Diego, CA.

Salloum, Alison, (2004). *Group Work with Adolescents After Violent Death: A Manual for Practitioners.* Taylor and Frances Publisher, New York, NY.

Spungen, Deborah (1998). *Homicide: The Hidden Victims.* Sage Publications, Inc., Thousand Oaks, CA.

Symonds, M. (1982). "Victim's Response to Terror: Understanding and Treatment." In F. Ochberb & D. Soskis (Eds.), *Victims of Terrorism* (pp.95-103). Westview, Boulder, CO.

Thompson, M.P., Norris, F.H. and Ruback, R. Barry (1998). "Comparative Distress Levels of Inner-City Family Members of Homicide Victims." *Journal of Traumatic Stress,* Vol. 11, No.2, 223-242.

Walsh, Froma (1998). *Strengthening Family Resilience.* The Guilford Publishers, New York, NY.

Wolin & Wolin (1993). *The Resilient Self: How Survivors of Troubled Families Rise Above Adversity.* Villard Books, New York, NY.

Zehr, Howard (2001). *Transcending: Reflections of Crime Victims.* Good Books, Intercourse, PA.

Zisook, S., Chentsova-Dutton & Shuchter, S. R. (1998). "PTSD Following Bereavement." *Annals of Clinical Psychiatry,* 10, 157-163.

Zoroya, Gregg (Oct. 11, 2014). "The Suicide Crisis." *USA Today.* Retrieved from http://www.usatoday.com/story/news/nation/2014/10/09/suicide-mental-health-prevention-research/15276353/.

About the Author

Connie Saindon is the author of Murder Survivor's Handbook: Real-Life Stories, Tips & Resources, which was honored with a Benjamin Franklin Gold Award in 2015. The book was judged as the best in the self-help category by the Independent Book Publishers Association.

Ms. Saindon is a licensed Marriage and Family Therapist and among the few specialists in the field of violent death bereavement. She founded the nonprofit Survivors of Violent Loss Program in San Diego, in 1998. It includes the website Violent Loss Resources (svlp.org). Her commitment to violent loss bereavement is related to the loss of her sister, aged 17, to homicide in 1961.

Her training includes the Restorative Retelling Model developed by Edward K. Rynearson, MD. She coauthored a preliminary study that showed significant decreases in symptoms using this model. She has provided program development, clinical services, training, and supervision of medical residents, interns, and clinicians.

Her research experience expanded by participation in two more studies published in Death Studies Journal (2013, 2014) as both a lead and contributing author. These studies cover 14 years worth of work, with results showing significant decrease in client symptoms related to traumatic grief, complicated bereavement, and post-traumatic stress.

Ms. Saindon is a frequent presenter at national conferences on this specialized topic. Her training programs have included online courses, one- and two-day trainings and retreats for professionals, peer and crime victim advocates. Presentations have included: American Psychiatry Association, American Association for Marital and Family Therapists, Texas Crime Victims Clearinghouse Conference, Violent Death Bereavement Society, National Center for Crime Victims, and Parents of Murdered Children. Course titles include: The Restorative Retelling Model, Violent Death and PTSD, and Violent Death: Fostering Resilience While Healing Wounds.

She is a contributing author of Violent Death, Resilience and Intervention Beyond the Crises, Edward Rynearson, editor, and has written articles on trauma as well as homicide for the Encyclopedia of Trauma, edited by Charles Figley.

Her current work includes providing consultation, speaking, and training. Contact her directly at csaindon@svlp.org.

When not pursuing her professional interests she may be found kayaking in the Atlantic or Pacific oceans, skiing, walking her dog, or taking photographs.

About the Editor

Larry M. Edwards is an award-winning author, editor, and investigative journalist. His book, *Dare I Call It Murder: A Memoir of Violent Loss*, won first place in the 2014 San Diego Book Awards for Best Published Memoir; the book was nominated for a Pulitzer Prize.

Mr. Edwards edited the 2015 IBPA Benjamin Franklin Gold Award winner (Self-Help), *Murder Survivor's Handbook: Real-Life Stories, Tips & Resources*, written by Connie Saindon.

Previously, he won Best of Show honors from the San Diego Press Club in 1994, 1997, 2004, and 2005, in addition to numerous other awards during his 25 years in journalism. Outside of writing and editing, he plays the fiddle in old-time music and bluegrass bands, and he is a historical reenactor. He lives in San Diego, California, with his birding-enthusiast wife, Janis Cadwallader.

Website: www.LarryEdwards.com.

Made in the USA
San Bernardino, CA
26 May 2019